A Strategy for Reading
Biblical Texts

Studies in Biblical Literature

Hemchand Gossai
General Editor

Vol. 29

PETER LANG
New York ‹ Washington, D.C./Baltimore • Bern
Frankfurt am Main • Berlin • Brussels • Vienna • Oxford

Johnson T. K. Lim

A Strategy for Reading Biblical Texts

PETER LANG
New York ‹ Washington, D.C./Baltimore • Bern
Frankfurt am Main • Berlin • Brussels • Vienna • Oxford

Library of Congress Cataloging-in-Publication Data

Lim, Johnson T. K.
A strategy for reading Biblical texts / Johnson T. K. Lim.
p. cm. — (Studies in biblical literature; vol. 29)
Includes bibliographical references.
1. Bible—Reading. I. Title. II. Series.
BS617 .K64   220.6'01—dc21   00-030646
ISBN 0-8204-5028-6
ISSN 1089-0645

Die Deutsche Bibliothek-CIP-Einheitsaufnahme

Lim, Johnson T. K.:
A strategy for reading biblical texts / Johnson T. K. Lim.
–New York; Washington, D.C./Baltimore; Bern;
Frankfurt am Main; Berlin; Brussels; Vienna; Oxford: Lang.
(Studies in biblical literature; Vol. 29)
ISBN 0-8204-5028-6

The paper in this book meets the guidelines for permanence and durability
of the Committee on Production Guidelines for Book Longevity
of the Council of Library Resources.

Printed in the United States of America

I dedicate this book to a wonderful friend
Evelyn Eng Noi Huay
whose exemplary life is a great source of
encouragement to me

Acknowledgments

I am grateful to my parents who have provided me opportunities to pursue my education at home and abroad as well as given me unfailing support in all my scholastic endeavours.

I want to thank Professor Edgar Conrad for reading the manuscript and giving some helpful comments and constructive critiques.

Special thanks must go to Drs Roland Chia, Tom Oey, Lilian Lim and Mr Andy Lie who have given me freely of their time in reading the entire manuscript as well as engaging me in a fruitful dialogue.

I have been blest by their friendships. Coming from diverse disciplines and theological traditions, they have helped to improve this monograph greatly. All shortcomings are mine.

I am also thankful to my ministry partners without whose unfailing support, encouragement and recognition of this vital topic, this monograph might not have seen the light of day. Thanks to Lindsay, Lilian and Tom for proofreading the entire manuscript.

Much of this research was undertaken while taking a break from my postgraduate studies. I want to thank my alma mater—Trinity Theological College in Singapore for giving me access to the library books as well as providing a serene place for my research.

Finally, I would like to express my appreciation to the editor Hemchand Gossai for accepting my work for publication in the *Studies in Biblical Literature* series.

Contents

Preface

In 1997, I published a monograph entitled 'The Sin of Moses and the Staff of God: A Narrative Approach' (*Studia Semitica Neerlandica* monograph series, 35; Assen: Van Gorcum) in which I attempted to solve one of, if not the most difficult puzzle in the Pentateuch according to the opinio communis of scholars. Finding an answer to this hermeneutical conundrum concerning the sin of Moses in Numbers 20:1–13 is as difficult as solving a Rubik's cube. The reason is that in the history of interpretation there has been thirteen different interpretive answers given to explain this enigmatic episode. Common sense seems to dictate that not all of the answers (or none for that matter) can be correct at the same time. If all of them were correct, then in that one short incident, Moses would have committed thirteen different sins. Fortunately, I did not have to add another sin to bring it to fourteen!

In any case, in that monograph I articulated and argued for a position using a narrative approach based on sound exegesis. This was supported by textual, intratextual and intertextual evidence within its canonical precincts. In my view, if my exegetical explication of the enigmatic episode in Num 20:1–13 is accepted,[1] it will help to explain several of the so called semantic difficulties and textual problems in that passage. It may also advance and give impetus to an ongoing debate on this Pentateuchal puzzle.

With regard to this present monograph, there are three foci:

1) to explain and expand in detail some of the hermeneutical principles used in elucidating that enigma in my previous monograph.
2) to explore some of the broader and wider but thorny issues in hermeneutics.
3) to explicate in depth the text immanent hermeneutical strategy in reading Biblical Texts with reference to the Old Testament. To achieve

this, I shall be formulating a theory of textuality which incorporates insights from modern linguistics as well as from literary criticism.

The title of this monograph has been crafted carefully and purposefully. I have deliberately chosen the indefinite article "a" rather than the definite article "the". This is to suggest categorically as well as to recognise broadly that there are competing hermeneutical strategies in reading any text. Each of the strategies has its strengths and weaknesses. In due course they will become my important conversation partners.

Having said that, it is my opinion that a text oriented reading strategy is exegetically viable and likely to reap maximum benefits with minimum problems in helping readers discern the message of the texts.

Hopefully along the way, I shall make a small but significant contribution to the hermeneutical debates as well as clearing up some of the muddy waters of hermeneutical marshes.

Johnson T. K. Lim
January 2000, Singapore
Soli Deo Gloria

Note

1   It is very heartening to know that a recent article by William H. C. Propp, 'Why Moses Could not Enter the Promised Land', in *Bible Review* 14/3 (1998):36–40;42–43 has again strengthened my thesis albeit with a difference—the identity of the staff. For a defense of the staff of Moses, consult my article, 'Whose Staff is it Anyway?' in *Biblische Notizen* 85 (1996):17–21. It is outside the purview of this monograph to discuss the sin of Moses. For additional insights, see my articles, 'A Fresh Perspective on a Familiar Problem', *Henoch* 19 (1997) 161–174 and 'Parallel Scripts, Paradigm Shifts', *Biblische Zeitschrift* 42/1 (1998) 81–90. For other related issues, please consult 'A Theology of Leadership with Special Reference to the Role of Moses in Numbers 20:1–13', *Church and Society* 3/1 (2000) 11–15 and 'A Puzzle in the Pentateuch?' *Jewish Bible Quarterly* (forthcoming).

Editor's Preface

More than ever the horizons in biblical literature are being expanded beyond that which is immediately imagined; important new methodological, theological, and hermeneutical directions are being explored, often resulting in significant contributions to the world of biblical scholarship. It is an exciting time for the academy as engagement in biblical studies continues to be heightened.

This series seeks to make available to scholars and institutions, scholarship of a high order, and which will make a significant contribution to the ongoing biblical discourse. This series includes established and innovative directions, covering general and particular areas in biblical study. For every volume considered for this series, we ask the question as to whether it will push the horizons of biblical scholarship. The answer must be yes for inclusion.

In this volume Johnson Lim explores the complex and challenging issue of biblical hermeneutics. It is Johnson's contention that a textual reading is not only viable, but essentially the sanest manner in which to process in biblical hermeneutics. Johnson builds his argument carefully and cogently by examining the many methodologies which have been used in biblical interpretation. While Johnson's particular orientation is clearly evangelical in nature, scholars from different perspectives will find this study extremely helpful and insightful, even when there is disagreement. It will have to be reckoned with. The horizon has been expanded.

Hemchand Gossai
Series Editor

Chapter One

By Way of Introduction

Can the notion of a sacred scripture be returned in an age of desacralization and dehierarchization, in an age where a text can be reduced to a microfiche or floppy disk (Fishbane 1989:128)?

1.1 Prologue

Recent publications on Hermeneutics are burgeoning. A proliferation of books and publication of new journals and periodicals have demonstrated substantially and unabatedly the importance of hermeneutics. This suggests that scholarly and popular interest in hermeneutics are here to stay. This should not come as a surprise as the Bible has always been a very important document for the community of readers.[1]

Current debates on hermeneutics centre on metahermeneutics—a discussion of hermeneutical theory rather than the development of principles for doing hermeneutics. Centuries of interpretations, methodologies and criticism have all contributed to the complexity of the issues. Questions that need to be asked include, what are the advantages of different methodologies for understanding a text? How about their relationships? Are they complementary, supplementary or contradictory? What methods can best help explain and interpret a text? Can a literary method which is text centred allow for language to interact with the world of the writer? Can an interdisciplinary approach enrich interpretation?

Within the ambit of conflict in interpretation, there are also the issues of meaning and methodologies. How does one discern meaning in the text? Is meaning discovered in the text or generated by the reader? Is meaning polyvalent or is there a limit to pluralism? Is authorial intention retrievable or irretrievable? Are all methods advocated by the different schools of thought for interpreting the Bible valid? With a plethora of competing interpretive strategies, how should one choose? What are some of the profound ramifications for understanding Scripture?

These are some of the paramount but thorny issues which I hope to explore and address in this monograph. In the light of continuing trends of postmodernism, we should reexamine some of the prevalent hermeneutical theories and ask which hermeneutical theory best addresses contemporary religious, ethical, social and political issues.

1.2 The Significance of Interpretation[2]

Within biblical academia, interpretation continues to be in a fluid and fermenting state. Since the 1950's there has been a significant and dramatic but complex shift. Hermeneutical fervour is at its highest peak as new books and periodicals continue to roll off the press. Like Joseph's coat of many colours, so are the interpretive theories ranging from pragmatic to abstract.

From a popular usage of the word 'hermeneutics' used in biblical studies, it has slowly and subtly seeped into other tributaries of academic disciplines. Many methodologies have been developed in a variety of fields for interpreting and understanding stories (eg. literature, psychology, sociology, philosophy, linguistics, and phenomenology).[3] Indeed, interpretation has become a common household word in almost every academic discipline. Today, when one speaks of interpretation, that word has to be qualified because of its complexities and the reformulation of older theories and promulgation of new interpretive theories.[4] Interpretation plays a vital role in the regulation of people's life and society's norms and is deeply rooted in the structure of human existence. Understanding and interpreting go together. Everything we do is in a sense an interpretive art. Mazzeo (1978:3) aptly accents this issue:

> As the occasions for the interpretation arise from the hiddenness of its cause and operations, so the need for interpretation of literature, philosophy, religion and art arises from the alienness conferred by historicity—the cultural changes which occur one time in our civilization or the sheer foreignness of an alien culture.

In biblical studies, its significance has been aptly highlighted by Barr (1993a:150):

> Central to modern study of the Bible has been the theme of *interpretation*. Almost all currents of scholarship emphasized it . . . Not only does the Bible have to be interpreted, but interpretation goes on within the Bible itself.[5]

Those Christian communities which have accorded the Bible a sacred status have a greater reason and urgency to handle interpretation correctly. Since to them the Bible is the Word of God,[6] it has eternal relevance. Therefore, it is incumbent on the interpreters to *rightly divide the word of truth*[7] so that the message proclaimed as a result of exegetical investigation may not be distorted or convoluted. The danger of distorting the word of God (2 Cor 2:4, 2 Peter 3:16) is ever prevalent.[8]

Strangely, one of the finest accolades conferred upon the Christians is the title *ahl al kitab* (People of the Book).[9] Ironically, though the Bible is our common heritage and the focal point of our faith, it has become a hotbed of controversies—none as hotly and persistently debated in ancient and contemporary setting as the approach to interpretation.[10] Central to the conflict in interpretation are the issues of meaning and methodologies. Perhaps, it is not an exaggeration to say that the Bible has become a 'killing field'.

1.3 Sacred Texts

Out of historical necessity, it is not uncommon for religious groups to establish a set of texts as authoritative for the sake of coherence or identity. By establishing a canon, it affirms the permanence of the sacred texts while at the same time denying continuity or dependence on other normative texts. The word canon connotes measure or rule which seeks 'to provide or protect coherence and identity by agreeing on a standard by which other texts can be judged' (Kort 1988:123).[11]

Moreover, it is brought on by the need of a religious community to protect itself from an alien context or to alienate those within the community who appear to promulgate doctrines or behaviour threatening the community's identity and coherence.

Sundberg (1964) points out that in the early church many texts were considered religiously authoritative that were not included in the canon.[12] Hence according to him a distinction needs to be made between 'Scripture' (a wider term for less securely fixed group of texts that operated within the church to edify and instruct but not in the canon) and canonical texts. Similarly, Barton (1997:157–158) following Sundberg observes that *Scripture* 'which results from the growth of writings perceived as holy', while *Canon* is that 'which represents official decisions to exclude from scripture works deemed unsuitable'. Hence, canon-making is intentionally a limited and limiting act. By design, it seeks to judge other texts.

Sacred texts (scriptures?) exist in every society which serve as reference points for ethical standards. They are important for the survival of the community.[13] How do texts become sacred? According to Detweiler

(1985), texts become sacred when a community perceives they possess divine authority. Some of the characteristics of a sacred text include, claims of divine inspiration as well as it contains revelatory of divinity, encoded revelation and religious rituals. A sacred text effects a transformation of lives and is evocative of divine presence.[14]

Interpretation of texts does change as society undergoes social changes. Sacred texts may become irrelevant due to their inaccessibility, chronological and linguistic hiatus, etc. When that happens new interpretive paradigms are developed. Part of the reason has to do with contextualising the texts to make them more relevant and contemporary. As Tracy (1981:102) writes:

> . . . only its constant reinterpretation by later finite, historical, temporal beings who will risk asking its question and listening, critically and tactfully, to its responses can actualise the event of understanding beyond its present fixation in a text.

1.4 Approaching the Texts

Our point of departure is that we should approach the Bible as *human script* and *divine scripture* rather than an either or option.

It is human because it was written by human authors in human language using conventional forms and structures. In other words, the Bible is a human script because it communicates 'to ordinary people in ordinary language and ordinary literature' (Vanhoozer 1986:92).

For certain communities the Bible is believed to be divinely inspired because the claims of the biblical writers are taken seriously. That is to say, having experienced 'the activity of the Spirit of God, they bring a transcendent divine word' (Goldingay 1994:201). Therefore, since these people wrote on behalf of God, they spoke God's message rather than their own, 'by extension God is the real author' (Holladay 1994:126).[15]

Gomes (1996:14) frames it this way:

> The Jews who gathered together these books from a whole range of their writings and called them 'scripture' did so in the firm conviction that God spoke through these human writings, and that these human writings brought the people of God nearer to God.

Scripture is 'expressive of divine will' because it is a depot and locus of divine revelation. Therefore, the message of the text can be appropriated to guide the reader's life. To put it in another way, to know God is to know his word in the text.[16]

Regardless of one's theory of inspiration, it must be admitted that the claims of divine inspiration cannot be easily dismissed.[17]

What are some of the profound and paramount implications of seeing the Bible as both human and divine?

First, the Bible is the work of divine and human partnership (2 Tim 3:14–16, 2 Peter 1:20–21). It is the Word of God in human words where divine activity and human activity intertwined. Ultimately, God who is the Author of Scripture is the *auctor primarius*. This means that what God means is what the author meant.

The Bible should be viewed not only 'as a catalog of God's utterances but primarily a communication of God—communication in the literal sense: God himself communes with us' (Maier 1994:55). This is made possible because 'of the fateful crossing from the ineffable and infinite plenitude of God to the wholly affable and finite features of human language' (Fishbane 1989:128). Hence, 'the Bible was given by God to people not as a mystical document written in secret codes to be understood only by the initiated but as a clearly understandable document that people can interpret with common sense' (Koivsto 1993:155).

Therefore, 'the idea of men and God working at cross-purposes may be accepted as a theoretical possibility but it goes against the fibre of scripture which argues for God's character to be untruthful'(Noll 1993:149–150).

Secondly, Scripture can be read like any other book. This means that the Bible may be read as literature. The use of linguistics and literary tools is necessary and useful in assisting in the comprehension of the text. Reading the Bible for aesthetic pleasure is therefore a legitimate enterprise. Since meaning is expressed in language, it is then through language that meaning is understood. Therefore, there is a place for a grammatical—lexical and linguistic understanding of the texts. As Johann Jakob Wettstein comments

> Just as we read the Holy Scriptures and secular laws—and all books, old and new—with the same eyes, so also should we employ the same principles for understanding the scriptures that we use in understanding other books.[18]

In my judgement, a general understanding of the Bible is possible without the Holy Spirit (see Matt 23:21; John 5:39; Acts 17:11; 2 Tim 3:14) by linguistically gifted non believers using linguistics to shed light on linguistic problems.

Nevertheless, I maintain that spiritual understanding is not possible for all the communities of readers (2 Cor 3:14; 4:3) because there is a place for *theologia regenitorium* as shown in Scripture (I Cor 2:10–16; 1 John 2:26–27). As Silva notes 'we must accept the principle that only the spirit of God knows the things of God' and 'only someone who has the spirit can expect to acquire a truly satisfactory understanding of Scripture' (Kaiser & Silva 1994:24). If we deny the validity of *hermeneutica sacra*, we are denying that 'there is any philological justifiable way in which biblical texts can be distinguished entirely from other texts' (Poland 1981:33). To put it in another way, when the Bible is simply read like any other book, 'its evocative power is lost without some recognition of the interplay of the religious horizon of the text with the religious horizon of the modern interpreter' (Lints 1993:227).

> Because it is a human book we cannot understand it unless we employ all types of biblical criticism to the full. But because it is also a divine book we must recognize that these tools are insufficient by themselves for us to grasp and apply its message. To do that we must have a humble mind and a heart open to the guidance of the Spirit.
>
> (Wenham 1989:89)

Since there is an interplay of human and divine activity, 'the Bible holds its rightful place only if we acknowledge that it is both the Word of God and human words' (Young 1990:21). Therefore, it is unwise to pit one against the other or to emphasise one over the other.[19] By so doing we can fall prey to interpretive errors.

Both aspects should not be overlooked and the tension needs to be maintained. Kiovsto (1993:159) insists that 'balanced biblical hermeneutics begins with the theological foundation that the Bible is both the Word of God and the word of men.'

1.5 The Power of Scripture

Scripture is a sign post to God who reveals himself in his word to the world. It is the word of God given to humanity. Through the presence of the text God continues to manifest Himself to us. As Wood (1981:41) frames it 'God's past dealings with his people has become God's self disclosure to the present readers through the text which functions as an instrument through which God enters into a relationship with us.' Historicality of Scripture is made possible through time and space continuum. In other words, 'an event of understanding proper to finite human beings has here found expression' (Tracy 1981:102). Moreover, 'it is not merely a book of history or a book of devotion but a library of writings of proven worth, self consciously composed, collected, and preserved as the repository of wisdom both human and divine' (Gomes 1996:15).

The universal appeal of the Bible has enabled it to remain *norma normans* because it addresses ancient and modern issues. It is a 'textual microcosm of our human religious travail' (Fishbane 1989:131). As a 'classic text' it exudes an *innere kraft* with the power to impact and transform receptive readers of the texts. In other words, 'to hear the Word of God is to be affected' and 'this Word, one's world and one's self cannot be the same' (Wood 1981:41).

The Bible is 'an inscription of infinite profundity, depth and power' (Fishbane 1989:44) containing a 'structure of reality ' (130) where 'divine reality may be approximated in the transcendental convergence of all interpretation literary as well as personal' (133) and where 'the images and language can shape our discourse, stimulate our moral and spiritual growth' (132).

As Addinall (1991:265) rightly claims:

> The Bible is a literary collection, made from a wide variety of sources over a long period of time. Whatever may have been the intentions of the sources, the collection is presented to us with the claim, implicit throughout and sometimes explicit, that we are being given information of the most profound importance concerning our life and the world in which we live.

The primary aim of the Bible is given not only for information but reformation and transformation of human lives and value systems.[20]

> The text is prior: the interpreter stands before it humbly and prays that through the scholarly methods and the questions with which he comes to the text, God's Word will be heard afresh. This is the exciting task to which the interpreter is called. But it is also a dangerous task: God's word sweeps away my comfortably secure presuppositions; it is a Word of judgement as well as of grace.
> (Stanton 1977:69–70)

Notes

1   I owe this phrase to Professor Conrad. The community of readers consists of scholars, academicians and laity who may be religiously or non religiously inclined.

2   For a helpful treatment of the history of interpretation, see Karlfied Froelich, *Biblical Interpretation in the Early Church* ((trans/ed; Philadelphia: Fortress, 1984); James L. Kugel and Rowan A. Greer, *Early Biblical interpretation* (Philadelphia: Westminster Press, 1986); Craig Evans and James A. Sanders (eds), *Early Christian Interpretation of the Scriptures of Israel: Investigations and Proposals* (England: Sheffield Academic Press; JSNTSup 148; 1997) and Robert Grant and David Tracy, *A Short History of the Interpretation* (London: SCM Press, enlarged and revised, 1984); Gerald Bray, *Biblical Interpretation: Past and Present* (Downers Grove, Illinois: Intervarsity Press, 1996) and Donald K. Mckim, *Historical Handbook of Major Biblical Interpreters* (Downers Grove: Intervarsity Press, 1998).
    See also David Norton, *A History of Bible as Literature* (Cambridge: Cambridge University Press, 1993).

3   For a good introduction to hermeneutical issues, consult Irena R. Makaryk (ed), *Encyclopedia of Contemporary Literary Theory* (Toronto: University of Toronto Press, 1993); Michael Payne (ed), *A Dictionary of Cultural and Critical Theory* (Oxford: Blackwell Publishers, 1996), Leland Ryken, James C. Wilhot and Tremper Longman (eds), *Dictionary of Biblical Imagery* (Downers Grove, Intervarsity, 1998) and John Hayes (ed), *Dictionary of Biblical Interpretation* (2 vols; Nashville: Abingdon, 1998).

4   For representative studies, see Roy B. Zuck (ed), *Rightly Divided: Readings in Biblical Hermeneutics* (Grand Rapids: Kregel Publication, 1996); Bruce Corley, Steve Lemke and Grant Lovejoy, *Biblical Hermeneutics: A Comprehensive Introduction to Interpreting Scripture* (Nashville, Tennessee: Broadman and Holman Publishers, 1996). Janice Capel Anderson and Stephen D. Moore (eds), *Mark and Method: New Approaches in Biblical Studies* (Minneapolis: Fortress Press, 1992); John Barton, *Reading the Old Testament: Method in Biblical Studies* (Louisville, Kentucky: Westminster John Knox, 1984; rev ed, [1996]); 'Postcolonialism and Scriptural Reading', *Semeia* 75 (1996); Jack Kuhatschek, *Applying the Bible* (Grand Rapids: Zondervan, 1998); Andre LaCoque and Paul Ricoeur, *Thinking Biblically: Exegetical and Hermeneutical Studies* (trans. David Pellauer, Chicago, 1998); George T. Montague, *Understanding the Bible: A Basic Introduction to Biblical Interpretation* (Paulist, 1997); Kwok Pui-Lan, *Discovering the Bible in the Non Biblical World* (Maryknoll, New York: Orbis Books, 1995); James W. Voelz, *What Does This Mean?: Principles of Biblical Interpretation in the Post-Modern World* (St. Louis: CPH, 1995); Stephen D. Moore, 'History after Theory? Biblical Studies and the New Historicism', *Biblical*

Interpretation : 298–299; R. Barry Matlock, 'Biblical Criticism and the Rhetoric of Inquiry', *Biblical Interpretation* 5:2 (1997):133–159; Donald K. Mckim (ed), *A Guide to Contemporary Hermeneutics* (William B. Eerdmans, 1986); Birger Gerhardsson, *The Ethos of the Bible* (trans. Stephen Westerholm; Philadelphia: Fortress Press, 1989); W. Edward Glenny, 'The Divine Meaning of Scripture: Explanations and Limitations' *Journal of the Evangelical Society* 38:4 (1995):481–500; Mikeal C. Parsons, '"Making sense of what We read" : The Place of Biblical Hermeneutics', *Southwestern Journal of Theology* 35:3 (1993):12–20; J. Cheryl Exum and David J.A. Clines, *The New Literary Criticism and the Hebrew Bible* (JSOTSup 143; England: Sheffield, 1993); Gale A. Yee (ed), *Judges and Method: New Approaches in Biblical Studies* (Minneapolis: Augsburg Fortress, 1995); Sharon D. Welch, 'Biblical Interpretation in Christian Feminist Ethics', *Studia Theologica* 51 (1997):30–43; J. Benton White, *Taking the Bible Seriously: Honest Differences about Biblical Interpretation* (Louisville, Kentucky: Westminster/John Knox Press, 1993); Stephen R. Haynes and Steven L. Mckenzie (eds), *To Each Its Own Meaning* (Louisville, Kentucky: Westminster/ John Knox Press, 1993); John Goldingay, *Models for Scripture* (Grand Rapids: Eerdmans, 1994); James DeYoung and Sarah Hurty, *Beyond the Obvious: Discover the Deeper Meaning of Scripture* (Gresham: Vision House, 1995); Tina Pippin, 'Ideology, Ideological Criticism, and the Bible' *Currents in Research* 4 (1996):51–78; P. E. Satterthwaite and D. F. Wright, *A Pathway into the Holy Scripture* (Grand Rapids: Wm. B. Eerdmans, 1994); Robert W. Yarborough, 'Variation on a Theme History's nth Great Hermeneutical Crisis', *Journal of the Evangelical Theological Society* 39:3 (1996):443–455; Harry Rand, 'The Limits of Literality, *Literature and Theology* 9:2(1995):117–134; Gerald Loughlin, 'Following to the Letter: The Literal Use of Scripture' *Literature and Theology* 9:4 (1995):370–382; D. Brent Sandy and Ronald L. Giese jr., *Cracking Old Testament Codes: A Guide to Interpreting the Literary Genres of the Old Testament* (Nashville: Broadman and Holman, 1995); Stanley E. Porter (ed), *Handbook to Exegesis of the New Testament* (Leiden: Brill, 1997); H. Raisanen, 'Liberating Exegesis?' 78:1 (1996):193–204; Luis Alonso Schokel, *A Manual of Hermeneutics* (England: Sheffield 1998); Wilhelm Egger, *How to read the New Testament: An Introduction to Linguistic and Historical-Critical Methodology* (Hendrickson, 1996); Russell Pregeant, *Engaging the New Testament: An Interdisciplinary Approach* (Minneapolis: Augsburg Fortress, 1995) especially 13–42 and Dan McCartney and Charles Clayton, *Let the Reader Understand: A Guide to Interpreting and Applying the Bible* (Bridgepoint, 1994); Stanley E. Porter and Thomas H. Olbricht (eds), *Rhetoric, Scripture and Theology: Essays from the 1994 Pretoria Conference* (JSNTSup, 131; England: Sheffield, 1996) and Stanley E. Porter and Thomas H. Olbricht, *The Rhetorical Analysis of Scripture: Essays from the 1995 London Conference* (JSNTSup, 146; England: Sheffield, 1997).

For more detailed studies on the different methodologies in reading the Bible, see individual *Guides to Biblical Scholarship* (Old and New Testament series) published by Fortress Press.

5   Author's emphasis.

6   Contrast Barr's (1973a:120) statement who claims, 'If one wants to use Word-of-
     God type of language, the proper term for the Bible would be Word of Israel,
     Word of some leading Christians,' in *The Bible in the Modern World* (NY: Harper
     & Row 1973) 120.

     However, as Brown (1981:21) argues 'the fact that the word of the Bible is
     human and time conditioned makes it no less "of God". In the Bible, God com-
     municates Himself to the extraordinary extent that one can say that there is some-
     thing *of* God in the words. All other works, patristic, Thomistic, and ecclesiastic
     are words *about* God; only the Bible is the *Word of God*,' in *The Critical Mean-
     ing of the Bible* (Great Britain: Geoffrey Chapman, 1981). Emphasis mine.
     Moreover Schneiders (1993:30) adds that 'the Bible can be called the Word of
     God because this metaphor identifies the text as potential mediation of symbolic
     revelation, that is, of encounter with the self disclosing God.'

     The affirmation that he Bible is the Word of God 'is not an empirical statement
     but faith affirmation' (ibid:19) because of our faith commitment we have a pro-
     pensity 'to find meaning in that affirmation and intellectual honesty demands that
     we try to make sense of this affirmation by rigorous use of all the resources'
     (ibid:30).

     In a similar vein, Fishbane (1989:44) maintains that 'the true metier of Scrip-
     ture is that it is an inscription of infinite profundity, depth and power—one truly
     worthy to be called a *Word of God*.'

7   See 2 Timothy 3:16

8   See for example Jim Hill and Rand Cheadle, *The Bible tells me So: Uses and
     Abuses of Holy Scripture* (New York: Doubleday, 1996).

9   This phrase appears a few times in the Qur'ān in suras 5:68, 29:45 etc. It is
     applicable to the Jewish people as well.

10   Other related issues include the nature of authority, ethics of interpretation and
     trustworthiness of the text which are beyond our purview. For an introduction,
     see Frederick Houk Borsch, *The Bible's Authority in Today's Church* (Valley
     Forge, Pennslyvania: Trinity Press International, 1993).

11   According to Brown (1994:76),

     A Canon is like a galaxy rather easily distinguishable from other objects in
     the night sky. Functionally, it exerts is own gravitational pull, a kind of inner
     drive that affects external bodies and also contributes to its own develop-
     ment. Like a galaxy it is composed of a vast and varying multiplicity of
     elements, a canon is dynamic, richly plural and pluriform. As a galaxy is
     nevertheless something of a unity, so a canon has enough unity and struc-
     ture to be one thing rather than another. At any given time, and from any
     given perspective, canon has a coarse and practical unity, though that unity
     is always differently construed from different perspectives.

12   According to Barr (1983b:54), 'in describing a canon in the making a three-stage
     organisation is generally assumed although a two-stage conception, using only
     the two terms, the Torah and the "Prophets" which to us are in the Writings, may
     well have been in the Prophets is gaining ground.'

13   Cf. 'Where the text is supreme, literature is treated with reverence,' *The Straits Times* Feb 12 (1994:16).

14   It is commonly generalised that the underlying motivation of religious leaders in ascribing sacrality to the texts, is for manipulation and control over the members of the community. This is debatable since every society with sacred texts faces different problems. Hence the need for individual case study.

15   See also Grant Osborne, *3 Crucial Questions about the Bible* (Grand Rapids: Baker Books, 1995).

16   Cf John McIntyre's (1994:384) words:

> When the Christian theologian reasons his way through to a conclusion of a mixed theological/non theological kind, he has to handle arguments, composed of warrants, backings, and rebuttals, which are themselves mixed in kind, and have to be judged one over against the other. Rarely, if ever, do such arguments present themselves in totally pure form, as either analytic or substantial. So, once again, we have to return to reliance upon the judgement of the theologian, who reaches his decision, not by some blind process of blind intuition, but through the assessment of the validity of the argument which come to him out of the fields which constitute his theological field (384).

See his essay in 'Historical Criticism in a History-Centred Value System' in Samuel Balentine and John Barton (eds.), *Language, Theology and The Bible: Essays in Honour of James Barr's Seventieth Birthday* (Oxford: Clarendon Press, 1994) 370–384.

17   For an excellent but recent introduction to issues such authority, inspiration and revelation, see Donald Bloesch, *Holy Scripture: Revelation, Inspiration and Interpretation* (Downers Grove: Intervarsity Press, 1994); Alice Ogden Bellis, 'Objective Biblical truth versus the value of Various Viewpoints : a False Dichotomy', *Horizons in Biblical Theology* 17:1 (1995):25–36 and Georges Florovsky, 'Revelation and interpretation' *Epiphany Journal* 11:2 (1991):23–35.

See also, Jack B. Rogers and Donald K. Mckim, *The Authority and Interpretation of the Bible: An Historical Approach* (NY: Harper and Row publishers, 1979); Howard Marshall, *Biblical Inspiration* (London: Hodder and Stoughton, 1982); L. William Countryman, *Biblical Authority or Biblical Tyranny?* (Valley Forge, Pennsylvania, 1994); James D. Smart, *The Interpretation of Scripture* (Philadelphia: Westminster Press, 1961) especially chapters 7 and 8; Douglas Farrow, *The Word of Truth and Disputes about Words* (Winona Lake, Indiana: Carpenter Books, 1987); Paul J. Achtemeier, *The Inspiration of Scripture: Problems and Proposals* (Philadelphia: The Westminster Press, 1980) and J. K. S. Reid, *The Authority of Scripture* (London: Methuen and Co., 1957).

18   Quoted by Werner Stenger, *Introduction to New Testament Exegesis*, trans. Douglas W Stolt (Grand Rapids: Wm B. Eerdmans 1993):1.

19   Contra William McKane, *A Late Harvest: Reflections on the Old Testament*
      (Edinburgh: T & T Clark, 1995) whose (over?) insistent emphasis on the human
      dimension of the Texts leaves the reader poorer.

20   Cf. the corrective statement of David Lochead (1977:83–84):

      . . . the insistence of the reformers on the freedom of conscience of the
      interpreter has led to a view of hermeneutics in which an interpretation is a
      matter of opinion of the individual and in which one opinion is as good as
      another. Against this, we need to insist that interpretation is not a matter of
      "opinion" but of *praxis*. Interpretation does not end when we draw "moral"
      of a text, *but when we act upon it* (Emphasis mine).

Chapter Two

The Current Climate in Hermeneutics

It was the best of times, it was the worst of times,
it was the age of wisdom, it was the age of foolishness,
it was the epoch of belief, it was the epoch of incredulity,
it was the season of Light, it was the season of Darkness,
it was the spring of hope, it was the winter of despair . . .
(Dickens 1859:14)

2.1 A Paradigm Shift

The term paradigm shift is popularised by Thomas Kuhn in his book, *The Structure of Scientific Revolutions* (1970). According to him, a paradigm[1]

> stands for the entire constellation of beliefs, values, techniques, and so on shared by the members of a given community. On the other, it denotes one sort of element in that constellation, the concrete puzzle—solutions which, employed as models or examples, can replace explicit rules as a basis for the solution of the remaining puzzles of normal science.
> (1970:175)

Essentially, the thesis of his book is that scientific achievements are made by quantum leaps rather than gradual steps. They are bound by past events and traditions. One salient feature of scientific progress is its revolutionary character whereby the relinquishment of one theoretical structure characterised by general assumptions and techniques adopted by a community is substituted for another equally incompatible structure. When anomalies emanate which cannot be explained and appear incompatible with an existing paradigm, extraordinary science emerges which trigger a scientific revolution thereby replacing an existing paradigm with a new one. During this process, traditional ideas are challenged and confronted. At the same time, the adherents of the old and new paradigm are involved in scientific skirmishes where either the scientists revert to existing paradigm and reserve anomalies for future research or a new alternative emerges. This so called crisis precipitates a paradigm shift.[2]

In a less technical sense, a paradigm may be defined as a mindset, model, frame of reference and lens through which we view and interpret data. It is a philosophical framework of concepts, and assumptions (including values, beliefs, prior information, predisposition, etc) operating subconsciously. What it does is to impose structure and patterns in the observation of data so that proper responsible management of data can take place. A paradigm shift is said to have occurred when the old paradigm with old sets of assumptions is rejected and a new one with different sets of assumptions is embraced. What are some of the broad but significant implications of Kuhn's research for hermeneutics?

1)   All of us come to a text with certain presuppositions and assumptions (proven and unproven) called paradigms influenced by past experiences. How a text is perceived is strongly influenced by our paradigms.

2)   These so called paradigms operate subconsciously but powerfully determine the way we think, act and read and ultimately form habits of behaviour.

3)   Texts can only be interpreted in the light of our previous assumptions which we cling to. That is to say we cannot absorb and understand new information except by relating to what we already know (presuppositions) through filtering it in a way that fits our preunderstanding.

4)   More often than not, it is our prior commitment to certain assumptions rather than strength of evidence that determines or shapes our conclusion.

5)   When a paradigm shift takes place and a new paradigm is embraced, we see the same texts in different light ways which yield new insights.

6)   Paradigms can be changed with time, experiences etc although some are more difficult than others. The reason is that human nature tends to resist change as well as certain deep attachments we have towards certain things.

7)   More often than not, for a paradigm shift to occur in our thinking requires a leap of faith or personal experiences rather than mere proofs.

2.2 Current Scene

Broadly speaking, in recent years, the biblical winds of change have been blowing incessantly, triggering a significant hermeneutical *perestroika* with regard to the text and the reader.

Moore (1989:xiii) perceptively assesses the current state of hermeneutics as an 'exciting and confusing time for biblical studies'. It is exciting because the hermeneutical landscape is undergoing a cataclysmic change like the map of Eastern Europe. As new hermeneutical super highways are being built with wider theory lanes, interpreters have an array of methodological arsenal to choose from the hermeneutical armoury which may make the task of interpretation easier. The monolithic tendency of yesteryears appears to have diminished as interdisciplinary studies gain momentum.[3]

On the other hand, it is also a time of confusion because as new theories multiply, the hermeneutical forest is choked with technically esoteric thickets of jargons which are overgrown with incompatibilities. One cannot help but get the feeling that reading books on hermeneutics today is like wading through a miasma of hermeneutical fog with only a small torch light. Added to that biblical and literary interpretation have grown more intricate and sometimes producing adverse results due to information overload. This led Silva to say 'exposure to contemporary theories of meaning and interpretation not only can prove dizzying; they can also create personal angst about the uncertainty of human experience' (Kaiser & Silva 1994:247).

The fundamental question that is intermittently asked is whether a harmonic convergence among all theories is possible. Does the churning out of more interpretive strategies guarantee accurate interpretation? Is sorting through a haystack of hermeneutical information just to find a methodological needle possible?

Biblical interpretation has now reached a developmental phase whereby a synthesis of traditional methodologies and contemporary theories is constantly being reviewed. Changes in recent developments have also enlarged the hermeneutical canon of interpretation. In the process they have opened the pandora's box of pluralism and relativism. Edgerton (1992) capsulizes it best when he says

> Interpretation is in crisis. So many questions which once seemed settled, so many foundations which once seemed secure, so many agreements which once seemed firm, have come apart. Issues which go to the bedrock of interpretation have opened deep fissures.

2.3 Hermeneutics

2.3.1 Traditional Hermeneutics

Historically speaking, the discipline of hermeneutics goes back to classical Greece and can be traced to Plato. Hermes who was the messenger between gods and mortals was called Hermenes, interpreter of God. What started out as a subdiscipline of biblical studies or jurisprudence has become a main discipline.

Traditionally, it was epistemologically concerned with the prescriptive aspects where principles, methods and guidelines were laid down. Its focal point was interpreting the texts correctly. Included in the system of interpretation are explanation, explication, and elucidation which can be subsumed under the category called exegesis.[4]

2.3.2 Contemporary Hermeneutics[5]

The word hermeneutic is used in the singular when reference is made to contemporary theory of interpretation dealing with a general theory of understanding/language. This was popularised by Fuchs & Ebeling with insights drawn from the philosophical disciplines of Husserl, Heidegger, Schleiermacher and others. Contemporary hermeneutics shift its focus from explanation (*Erklarung*) to understanding (*Verstehen*). Both the reader and the text become conversational partners engaging in a dialogical encounter resulting in a fusion of horizons[6] (*Horizontsverschmelzung*) which is 'not fixed but moves with us and is the context whereby we understand things in their relationship' (Gadamer 1975:151). This merger 'is an active and meaningful engagement between the interpreter and the text in such a way that the interpreter's own horizon is re-shaped and enlarged' (Thiselton 1980:19).

To understand a text truly, the parts must be interpreted in light of the whole and vice-versa resulting in a *hermeneutical circle*[7] which is the constant going back to and fro between the interpreters and the text. As both horizons are merged, the interpreter enters the historical process of tradition and unites with the "world of text" resulting in a new world of meaning. In that moment of encounter, meaning takes place and as both horizons intersect, a common understanding/empathy takes place. Therefore, understanding takes place 'as we place ourselves within a process of tradition in which the past and present are constantly fused' (Gadamer 1975:258). In other words, the fusion of two horizons (reader's and the text's) where the past and present are intertwined leads to understanding. This then leads to self understanding (*Selbstverständnis*) which is a 'rediscovery of the I in the Thou' (Buber's dictum). However, it must be remembered that before a proper fusion can take place there must be distanciation and that 'understanding is subject to ideological bias and can never be exhaustive' (McCarthy 1992:219–224). As Thiselton (1980:445) articulates,

> The hermeneutical goal is that of a steady progress towards a fusion of horizons. But this is to be achieved in such a way that the particularity of each horizon is fully taken into account and respected. This means both respecting the rights of the text and allowing it to speak.

Reading is not to get information but to cause an event (*Ereignis*). A text has no meaning apart from the interpreter. In their theory of language, the role of an interpreter is reversed and the interpreter listens instead of receiving. Through language, the language event (*Sprachereignis*) challenges the interpreter toward an authentic human existence. The issue in contemporary hermeneutics is not 'how we understand a text but what we do with it' (Lochhead 1979:391). In other words, comprehension of a text is equated with the ability to use it for personal and practical application.

Contemporary hermeneutics seeks to bridge the gap between the reader and the text and modes of experience (*Erfahrungsweisen*) in the modern context. By relating what the text meant in its ancient context to what the text means now in its modern context, common understanding (*Einverständnis*) develops. Therefore it sees interpretation not as 'boring a shaft into the text to extract its abundance of wealth, [but] it sees the process as an interaction between the text and interpreter' (Aageson 1993:8).

Since it is more concerned with the descriptive aspects of interpretation, 'it has widened the scope to include epistemological and ontological dimensions where questions such as—what is the being of the entity which has an understanding of itself and the world?' (Lategan 1992:149).

2.3.2.1 Contribution

Contemporary hermeneutics places strong emphasis on the semantic autonomy of the text. Once the text becomes public domain, its sense is no longer related to the referents. A text does not contain meaning but it mediates meaning. Also the text reveals a particular understanding of existence. As the text is seen as autonomous from the author, it is open to a new relationship with the reader. As both interact a new world of meaning emerges.

The role of preunderstanding (*Vorverständnis*) is very much highlighted in contemporary hermeneutics. Human understanding of texts is filtered through an interpretive framework which is experientially conditioned and founded upon life relationship (*Lebensverhältnis*). Therefore, it is not possible to read a text without being influenced by our presuppositions. In fact it is very essential for understanding the text. Preunderstanding (prejudice?) cannot be eliminated in the process of interpretation. Although, it can be deepened, modified and corrected by the distanciation between the reality of the text and the reader. One of the ways is to respect 'the world of the text in its otherness'.

Another area of contribution by contemporary hermeneutics is the assertion that total objectivity is an impossibility. It also emphasises the historicality and common humanity of the text and interpreter. That is to say 'human consciousness cannot transcend its own time-bound milieu' (Noll 1993:138). Its emphasis on dialectical encounter in reading and the particularity of the text and interpreter are to be valued.

The role of the reader is given (too) much prominence whereby there is a shift from *correct* reading to *creative* reading. Correct reading is no longer given legitimacy since meaning is generated by the reader. Everyone brings a particular interpretive scheme when reading a text thereby generating new meaning and creating a new text. As a result of indeterminacy of meaning 'what is true' for me becomes what is true '(Conn 1988:194).

One of the problems (weaknesses) of contemporary hermeneutics is its uncontrolled subjectivism resulting in what the text says has no bearing of what it actually meant. Instead, the text is taken as object and subject whereby in confronting the text we ourselves are in turn being confronted. There's also much emphasis given to subjectivity and relativity.

Contemporary hermeneutics are too quick to dismiss any methods of interpretation but for the wrong reason. This is partly due to a paranoia of domesticating the text and dictating in advance what a text ought to say.[8]

2.3.3 Postmodern Hermeneutics

A new type of hermeneutics called (post)modern hermeneutics is already becoming a familiar term in the arena of biblical interpretation. Postmodernism[9] is becoming or has become a keyword in art, culture, architecture, literature, etc. It is claimed by many that we are not only approaching the end of the twentieth century/modern era but the beginning (continuation?) of an era called postmodern.[10] Postmodernism can be explained in part by the dramatic developments occurring throughout culture and society like media explosion, political shifts and upheavals, new experiences' (Best and Kellner 1991:ix).

It is generally recognised that a shift from truth to fiction (and narrative) and the demise and collapse of science, politics, religion, and Enlightenment ethos marks the beginning of postmodernism.[11]

Postmodernism as a term may be viewed as a 'cultural epoch through which we are living and as a development in thought that represents a thoroughgoing critique of the assumptions of Enlightenment in terms of art, literature, culture, many aspects of society, the discourses of modernity and their foundation in notions of universal reason' (Hawthorn 1994:119–124).

2.3.3.1 Terminology

What is postmodernity? Lyotard's classic definition is 'simplifying to the extreme . . . incredulity toward metanarratives' (1984:xii–xiv).[12] It is incredulous toward metanarratives (big ideas) because 'they provide a narrative foundation for our way of life by defining and enforcing realities' (Vanhoozer 1995:405). For postmodernists language is seen as an instrument of ideology and power; it is an ethics of resistance to metanarrative (a story that explains all stories or theory of reality); distrusting any voice that speaks for others or with finality; no innocent reading since all reading is influenced by social power; and that truth is perspectival and community based rather than universal (ibid:6–7). 'There is nothing outside the text; all is textual play with no connection with original truth' (Derridian dictum) catches the spirit of postmodernism. Simply put, the world of postmodernism is 'where everything is possible and almost nothing is certain' (Havel).[13]

2.3.3.2 Tenets

Postmodernism represents the logical conclusion of the Enlightenment and its foundational assumptions (eg rejection of objectivity of knowledge, autonomous knower, etc.). It seeks to eliminate all philosophies (traditional and modern) of the Greeks like Aristotle and Plato as well as Christianity (reason and revelation) especially in the area of epistemology. Philosophically, a postmodernist 'cannot accept any system of knowledge as absolute or foundational; subject or knowledge that is a unified totality and any mystifying claims that any intellectual discourse is disinterested or pure' (Adam 1995:15). It rejects 'modern assumptions of social coherence and notions of causality in favour of multiplicity, plurality, fragmentation and indeterminacy' (Best and Kellner 1991:4).

Postmodern theory represents a shift from positivism and objectivity to subjectivity. One common denominator of postmodern thinking is that it seeks to 'problematize legitimation, the means by which claims about truth or justice or reality are validated or rejected' (Adam 1995:5). Therefore 'it is suspicious of any claim of universality, completeness and challenge the supremacy of traditional interpretation as enactments of domination and powerplays' (Postmodern Bible 1995:2-3). Hence, it seeks to undermine the stability of meaning in a text and raises doubts concerning the capacity to achieve clarity of the text ultimately.

Postmodernism argues that the existence of an objective reality[14] (confidence display by modernism) can no longer be believed. The seemingly objective reality of interpreting texts are 'really expressions of power (political, economical, scholarly or religiously)tend to justify their power by appealing to objective analyses that support the structured world they operate' (Keegan 1995:1). In other words, 'because truth is non rational, there are other ways of knowing, including through the emotions and the institution, thereby 'the human intellect as the arbiter of truth is dethroned' (Grenz 1995:94).

Postmodernism generally attacks objectivism where meaning of a text is given a privileged character and absolutes.[15] Moreover, a subjectivism that equates the meaning of a text with understanding the mind of the author is not spared either. It has also been argued forcefully that 'no reading is innocent and that every reading is ideological and that what the text meant and how it means are inseparable from what we want it to mean, from how we will it to mean' (Postmodernist Bible 1995:4, 14).

Postmodernism hermeneutics recognise the 'legitimacy of diverse readings from a text but denies the idea of logocentrism which advocates that language communicates a centre or the presence of an order or logos that is beyond language' (Keegan 1995:5). Elements like indeterminacy, polyvalency and subjectivity are necessary in the study of reality. It maintains those who take an objective approach to the facts of experience lead to a paradoxical conclusion.

Since objective truth is not accessible and meaning does not reside in external reality or texts but in the interpreter, 'pluralism is a necessary and desirable cultural and philosophical phenomenon' (Henry 1995:41). In a word, a postmodern reader is 'incredulous towards metanarratives, oriented towards reading formation rather than readers and texts, unauthorized, indifferent to time and time conditioning, and transgressive' (Adam 1995:22).

In sum, the five basic tenets of postmodernism according to James Sire are:[16]

1) Things and events do not have intrinsic meaning. There is only continuous interpretation of the world.
2) Continuous examination of the world requires a contextual examination; we ourselves are part of the context.
3) Interpretation depends not on the external text or its author, but on the relative viewpoint and particular values of the interpreter.
4) Language is not neutral, but relative and value laden.
5) Language conveys ideology

2.3.3.3 Characteristics

Postmodernism is predisposed to recognise more complexities existing between the interaction of the reader and the text because of the various factors (eg social, economic, institutional, etc.) vying for reader's attention and allegiance. Therefore, the reader-text interaction is undermined and cannot be used as a reliable foundation for objective interpretation because 'the reader encounters several different versions of the "text", which shimmer and shift, chameleon-like, into further texts' (Adam 1995:18).[17]

A postmodernist will present knowledge (eg encyclopedia) as illusory or nightmarish. Instead of explaining a work, they will sketch a series of relations among certain topics. Rather than claiming privileged access to truth, they will claim to have provided a provocative reading. A post modernist will begin with an insignificant or irrelevant quotation as a starting point. In other words, 'postmodernism is wilfully transgressive; it defies the boundaries that restrict modern discourses to carefully delimited regions of knowledge' (Adam 1995:22).

One problem with postmodern hermeneutics readers is that they 'will not respect the shadow of any disciplinary Father who would hold them accountable to the laws of that particular field of knowledge or communication' (Adam 1995:22). Therefore all rules of interpretation are considered as provisional guide and not stringent or foundational laws. Rules are simply transferred habits and styles of mentors. Hutcheon (1989:1–2) is on target when he describes postmodernism as a

> Phenomenon whose mode is contradictory, and a nudging commitment to doubleness because it manages to install and reinforce as much as undermine and subvert the conventions and presuppositions it appears to challenge.

According to Bauman (1992:272), 'postmodernity is modernity coming to terms with its own impossibility; a self-monitoring modernity, one that consciously discards what it was once unconsciously doing.' Consider the metaphor of Culler (1981:118) who says that 'postmodern critics rub the texts together to see what sparks will fly and what will perhaps catch fire.' The confession of Foucault best summarises a postmodern reader: 'A nightmare has pursued me since childhood: I have under my eyes a text that I can't read, or of which only a tiny part can be deciphered. I pretend to read it, but I know I am inventing'(quoted by Moore 1994:112).

According to Eagleton,

> We are now in the process of wakening from the nightmare of modernity, with its manipulative reason and fetish totality, into the laid back pluralism of the postmodern, that heterogeneous range of life styles and language games which has renounced the nostalgic urge to totalise and legitimize itself.[18]

In biblical studies, Postmodernism hermeneutics find expressions in deconstructionism and some reader response criticism.

2.4 Cultural Shifts

2.4.1 Modernity to Postmodernity

The infrastructure of the epistemology of the Enlightenment is now crumbling. The phenomenon of pluralism (eg world religions, diverse ideologies) world wars, breakdowns of authority structures, scientific positivism, etc. has broken the stranglehold of western hegemonistic and monopolistic tendencies.

The so called objective certitude of modernity of the 19th century has been seriously but successfully challenged by Einstein's theory of Relativity, Heinsenberg's 'principles of uncertainty' in Quantum physics, and Kuhn's paradigm of scientific facts as theory laden, etc.

This cultural shift impacted every area of scientific disciplines. In biblical studies, the 'assured results of historical criticism' has given way to relativity and uncertainty. The shift in the epistemology of hermeneutics, biblical and literary studies is the result of the impact of postmodernity.

As Lints (1993:197) observes,

> The fundamental methodological shift in the present era has been a movement away from a detached, disinterested, scientific and critical theology toward a subjective, reader response, literary and critical theology.

2.4.2 Differences between Modernity and Postmodernity

Modernity values absolutes, universal, unified and total knowledge while postmodernity talks of relativity, locality and particularity of knowledge (Adam 1995:15–16). Modernity's goal is essentially the discovery of 'the theory of everything' whereby everything can be explained by one theory. By so doing they hope to give 'a unified explanation, a grand theory that would find a rational place for everything and put everything in its rational place' (Vanhoozer 1995b:4–5). Vanhoozer sees the emphasis of modernity in global narratives, purpose, design and hierarchy in the natural and social worlds; transcendence of the knowing subject, of reason; and substitute God the father with Reason playing the role of transcendent authority. On the other hand, postmodernity emphasises local narratives, expects rule of chance, desire and anarchy; stresses immanence and substitute for the Holy Spirit—the more diffuse horizontal and non hierarchical presence of the divine in the world.

To put it simply, modernism accents Rationalism, Ultimate Truth, Uniqueness of Individuals, Principles and Absolutes. Whereas postmodernism accentuates Relativity, Uncertainty and Perspectivity. It celebrates the demise of Truth and denial of any Universal Truth or Morality. Furthermore, individuals are not significant but are constructs of social forces—race and gender.

Toulmin (1990) characterises modernity as emphasising what is written rather than oral (reliability equals written); particular to universal (real truth equals truth everywhere); local to general (real truth had to be the same from locale to locale) and from the timely to the timeless (reality equals unchangeability). Postmodernism on the other hand would be a reversal of modernity that is from written to oral; universal to particular; general to local and timeless to timely.[19]

Creatively put, modernity is best represented by Descartes and postmodernity is best represented by Derrida. In the words of Vanhoozer (1995b:3–7),

Descartes decentred God and divine revelation by making the knowing subject and Reason to be the source of truth. Derrida decentred the knowing subject and Reason by arguing that language and rhetoric are more fundamental. Derrida is the stowaway on Descartes' voyage to certainty, a hermeneutic hitman! Whereas Descartes believed he had landed and struck bedrock-his consciousness, Derrida denies that. He doubts Reason's ability to achieve a 'totalizing' discourse, that is a universal explanation of some aspect of reality. As a deconstructor or undoer, he wants to undo the covenant between language and reality and logocentricism-the belief that language can be used to map reality and that consciousness can mirror cosmos.

Therefore, 'if modernism represented a desperate effort to have art and culture fill the void created by the decline of the religion in the West, then postmodernism stands as the affirmation of the void, as the declaration of the impossibility of ever filling it' (Lundlin 1993:3-4). [20]

2.5 Hermeneutical Shifts

2.5.1 Historical to Literary

The 1920's witnessed the popularity of the historical critical approach[21] which became standard in biblical exegesis in the fifties and sixties. But the beginning of the seventies saw the development of a synchronic approach where attention is focused on the linguistic and literary forms/ structures, semantic and syntactic aspects of the text (eg narratology, rhetorical criticism, intertextual, semiotics, ideology criticism, structuralism making inroads into biblical exegesis) rather than its historical development and reconstructions. From a primarily historical critical perspective, the pendulum has swung to a literary (critical) perspective.[22] This is a very significant but major shift that has occurred in Biblical Interpretation which biblical studies has welcomed, hesitantly at first but then more readily after a century of domination by historical criticism (Long 1994:149).

Much emphasis is placed not on prehistory of the text but the final form because meaning lies in the text, not behind it. That is to say that theological meaning is not grounded in history behind the text or in its stages of development but rather in the text itself. This in turn helps to free the text from the mooring of the author's historical and psychological experiences. Hence, the final text is to be interpreted in its own right. Attention is also being paid to the compositeness and integrity of the text as well as in the literary function of the text, its artistic structure, forms of expression rather than some historical referents residing outside the text and divergent sources.[23]

This shift from historical to literary has generated interest in internal science which seeks its rules and principles within the literary work itself rather than external science—which seeks sources external to text. In other words, its focus has shifted from source to discourse and from genesis to poetics. Poetics is explained as the 'science of literature that seeks to find the building blocks of literature and the rules by which they are assembled' (Berlin 1983:15).

2.5.2 Text to Reader

There is also a shift in hermeneutics where the reader has priority over the text. This is due to the influence of (post)modernism. A (post)modern hermeneutic reader believes objectivity in interpretation is impossible. There is no determinate meaning in the text. Meaning is not discovered but generated by the reader. The aim of reading is for the reader to manipulate and impose his worldview and ideology over the world of the text.

Emphasis is placed on the reader and text as partners in the enterprise of reading. According to Keegan (1985), 'a literary work (text) is only a potential but becomes a reality when the two poles (reader and the text) are operative.' To put it in another way, the text is a *virtual entity* that is capable of existing itself but does not yet exist. It only becomes a reality when a reader actually reads a text. The reader, acting like a potter, fashions the lump of clay into whatever sizes and shapes he so desires. The text may determine the reader's response but because it is full of gaps, it is the reader's responsibility to fill it. What the text was eventually becomes different from what a text is. More weight is given to the reader stressing his interests and concerns but little weight is given to its textual constituents.

In other words, eisegesis rather than exegesis is the order of the day whereby one enters the text with new questions to produce new meaning rather than bringing meaning out like taking an object out of the box.[24] What is more important is what the text means now more than what it meant then.

2.5.3 Summary

The shift in contemporary hermeneutics orientation is towards the reader and a rejection of the idea of an organic text. A text is not considered a unified nor autonomous object but a set of relations with other texts. The shift from the text to the reader involves studying the conditions of meaning rather than meaning itself. To put it simply, 'the birth of the reader is the death of the author' (Barthes' famous phrase).

According to the reader centred approach, a text is incapable of communicating truth about any objective reality. It has a range of possible meaning but not the meaning because reality can be interpreted from different perspectives of the reader. Hence one reader's meaning is considered as proper as the other reader however incompatible because there is no final textual meaning. What we have is not objective knowledge or reality but a linguistic construct because language is viewed as metaphorical and a surfeit of over exact meaning.

All meaning is subjectively bound with the reader rather than with the text. Words are said to have other words as their referents. It is the reader that gives meaning to the text since all exegesis is eisegesis.

A postmodern oriented hermeneutics reader resists any claim of textual meaning that seeks to be authoritative or absolute. Any attempt to fix the meaning of the text is interpreted as a covert attempt to impose authoritarian rule on the reader. There is no universal interpretation of the biblical texts but only local meanings because the reader is unable to transcend his or her social location. True objectivity is impossible because objectivity is a human construct.To name something evokes expression of power and thereby does violence to what is named. Knowledge is not culturally neutral but rather historically and culturally conditioned. Since Scripture is culturally originated, it can therefore be rejected by readers in a different social setting. Hence, pluralism is valued because it is a liberating force.

In the light of contemporary hermeneutics (modern and postmodern), traditional exegesis needs to be evaluated. It is a challenge that must be faced.[25]

Notes

1   Critics have pointed out correctly that Kuhn's usage of the word paradigm has been inconsistent and fuzzy. One critic has even called it "scientifically perspicuous and philosophically obscure". Kuhn has conceded on this point and he later clarifies in his post-script that *disciplinary matrix* (1970:182) and *exemplars* (1970:187) are more precise terms. However, the use of paradigm continues to be widely and loosely used.

2   For more details, see Kuhn (1970:1–4; 35–42; 109–110; 198–204). See also Poythress (1988) and Suppe (1973:459–482).
    Contrast Barton (1993:13) who insists that to use the phrase historical-critical paradigm is 'to suggest that biblical criticism is either dead anyway, or an option that the discriminating scholar might do better to shrug off' and cannot appeal to the authority of Kuhn. Cf. Ryken (1993:49) who remarks that 'the current literary study of the Bible reflects a paradigm shift for both biblical and literary scholars.' Also Klein, Bloomberg and Hubbard (1993:425) state that 'today, however, many Bible scholars particularly those outside of evangelical circles, are calling nothing less than a paradigm shift in hermeneutics.' Hence, to describe the current hermeneutical landscape as paradigm shifts is acceptable.

3   Although interdisciplinary research is not always easy, it can be fraught with an air of excitement of discovering possibilities of new insights. In my opinion one should take advantage of the new insights and results obtained from other disciplines in order to make progress.

4   Essentially, hermeneutics means the theory of interpretation for understanding a text; exegesis is the practice of examining a text to determine its meaning in its original context; exposition is drawing out the implications of the meaning in the text for contemporary context; and homiletics is the science and art of preaching.

5   For an excellent summary and discussion of contemporary Hermeneutics, see Bernard C Lategan, 'Hermeneutics,' in *Anchor Bible Dictionary*, vol 3 (NY: Doubleday, 1992) 149–154; Moises & Silva (1994:229–248); Richard E. Palmer, *Hermeneutics: Interpretation Theory in Schleiermacher, Dilthey, Heidegger, and Gadamer* (Evanston: Northwestern University Press, 1969) and Kurt Mueller-Vollmer, *The Hermeneutics Reader* (New York: Continuum, 1992) and Robert Detweiler and Vernon K. Robbins, 'From New Criticism to Poststructuralism: Twentieth-Century Hermeneutics', in Stephen Prickett (ed), *Reading the Text: Biblical Criticism and Literary Theory* (Oxford: Blackwell, 1991):225–280.
    For the contribution of some of the luminaries in Contemporary Hermeneutics like Gadamer, Schleiermacher, Heidegger, see the *magnum opus* of Anthony C Thiselton, *The Two Horizons: New Testament Hermeneutics & Philosophical Description with Special Reference to Heidegger, Bultmann, Gadamer and Wittgenstein* (Exeter: Paternoster 1980) and *New Horizons in Hermeneutics: The Theory & Practice of Transforming Biblical Reading* (Grand Rapids:

Zondervan, 1992) and Tom Rockmore, 'Gadamer, Rorty and Epistemology as Hermeneutics', *Laval Theologique et Philosophique* 53:1 (1997):27–41.

6   The metaphor *horizon* means the range of our understanding, intention and question.

7   Some prefer to call it "hermeneutical spiral" because it recognises a dialectical relationship between the text and the interpreter, yet indicating a forward movement towards the focal point of a fuller understanding.

8   Some of the differences between traditional and contemporary hermeneutics may be explained this way: The former sees interpretation as an enterprise. It is more interested in the nature of interpretation (eg methods, meaning of the text, etc.). The author of the text or the text itself is accented. It treats the text as *object* standing "under" us.

   On the other hand, contemporary hermeneutics see interpretation as a dialectic encounter between the reader and the text. It is more interested in existential understanding. The reader is accented. It treats the text as *subject* standing "over" us.

9   For a brief introduction to this subject, see Lim (1997):21–23.

10 For an excellent bibliographical data on understanding Postmodernism and its impact on biblical studies, see Lim (1997) page 22, footnote 40.

   Is Postmodernism a cause for celebration or a cause for alarm? Is it to be given a big welcome or a guarded one? For a sane discussion of these issues and their impact, see Paul Lakeland, *Postmodernity: Christian Identity in a Fragmented Age* (Minneapolis: Fortress Press, 1997) and Roger Lundlin (ed), *Disciplining Hermeneutics: Interpretation in Christian Perspective* (Leicester, England: Apollos, 1997); John Reader, *Beyond all Reason: The Limits of Postmodern Theology* (Aureus Publishing, 1997).

11 On the other hand we need to recognise that there is no set unified post modern theory.

12 The term postmodernism can be used in three ways: First, as a reference to the 'cultural epoch through which we are living and largely viewed in apocalyptic terms'. Second, 'as an aesthetic practice which is seen variously as co-extensive with the commodified surfaces of this culture or as a disruption of its assumptions from within'. Third, 'as a development in thought that represents a thoroughgoing critique of the assumptions of Enlightenment or the discourses of modernity and their foundation in notions of universal reason' (Waugh 1992:3).

13 See Vaclav Havel, *The Art of the Impossible: Politics as Morality in Practice* (Alfred A. Knopf, 1997).

14 Foundationalism says that there are some absolutes that knowledge can be based upon and certain foundational or basic facts to which thoughts can appeal. Meaning is sought in the free associations of words.

15 See Michael LaFargue, 'Are Texts Determinate? Derrida, Barth, and the Role of the Biblical Scholar,' in *Harvard Theological Review* 81 [1988]: 341–57).

16   Quoted by Dockery (1995:14). Cf. James W. Sire, *The Universe Next Door* (Downers Grove, Illinois: Intervarsity Press, 1997, [third edition]) especially pages 172–191.

See Adam (1995:5) who suggests three characteristics of postmodernism. Postmodernism is anti foundational because it refuses to acknowledge any premise as privileged starting point for establishing claims to truth. It is antitotalizing in that it assumes and suspects that any unified theory of everything is suppressing counter examples. It is demystifying to show that all ideals/claims that certain assumptions are natural are grounded in ideology, economic or political interest.

17   See also Loren Wilkinson, 'Hermeneutics and the Postmodern Reaction Against "Truth", Elmer Dycke (ed), in *The Act of Reading Bible* (UK Paternoster Press, 1996):114–147; Craig Bartholomew, 'Post/Late? Modernity as the Context for Christian Scholarship Today,' *Themelios* 22.2 (1997):25–38; Kevin Vanhoozer, 'Mapping Evangelical Theology in a Postmodern World' *Evangelical Review of Theology* 22:1 (1998): 5–27; Philip R. Davies, 'Biblical studies in a Postmodern Age', *Jian Dao* 7 (1997):37–55; Stanley Grenz, 'Christian Integrity in a Postmodern World' *Vox Evangelica* (1997): 7–26; Walter Brueggemann, 'Biblical Theology Appropriately Postmodern', 27:1 (1997):4–9; Leander E. Keck, The Premodern in the Postmodern World,' *Interpretation* 50:2 (1996):130–141 and Graham Ward, *The Postmodern God: A Theological Reader* (Oxford: Blackwell Publishers, 1997).

18   Cited in *Tomorrow is a Another Country* (London:Longdunn Press, 1996): 9–10.

19   See Stephen Toulmin's book, *Cosmopolis: The Hidden Agenda of Modernity* (New York: Free Press, 1990): 30–35; 186–192.

20   The final result of scientific positivism is the end of modernity ushering into postmodernity.

21   Actually it was well underway in the eighteenth and nineteenth century.

22   The popularity of a literary approach stems from the 'teaching of Bible in college literature courses and the work of liberal scholarship,' claims Ryken (1993:57). Literary criticism is a by-product of modernity, while the new (er) literary criticism is the by-product of postmodernity. Literary criticism affirms the coherence and unity of biblical material.

On the other hand, new(er) literary criticism subverts the final form of the text. Some of its tenets are: the bible is to be read politically which means reading below the surface; the presence of contradictions is to be welcomed because textual struggles help to illuminate the text; there is no centre (ie no single story); it does not allow one overriding purpose to overshadow other possible positions that other tradents might have contributed; the final editor is not given the final/absolute say in what is the centre, important part of the work; they seek those aspects that have been marginalised by the editor and give it a voice; opposition to bifurcation (good/evil; insider/outsider/righteous and unrighteous.they make the good bad and the bad look good. Abraham (insider show weakness, hypocrisy while the outsider showed spiritual understanding (harlot). See J. Cheryl Exum and

David J. A. Clines, *The New Literary Criticism and the Hebrew Bible* (JSOTSup, 143; Sheffield: JSOT Press, 1993).

23   For a general overview and understanding of historical criticism with reference to the source theory, see Lim (1997) especially pages 7–27. See footnote 5 for an extensive bibliography.

24   See S. Croatto, *Biblical Hermeneutics: Towards a Theory of Reading as the Production of Meaning* (Maryknoll: Orbis, 1987).

25   Lundlin (1993:4–6) makes an interesting claim concerning some of the overlapping concerns between orthodox christianity and postmodernism. We summarise his views.

Both camps are skeptical of the claims of reason and imagination; critical of the confidence of the western mind to know truth with scientific certainty and suspicious about the faith placed in the power of the self conscious intentions to control and direct the course of history.

However, where they differ is the conclusion about the nature of truth. Whereas the postmodernists will abandon the search for truth altogether and instead turn to a "therapeutic understanding of the human experience". A therapeutic culture is where questions concerning the meaning of truth, the existence of God, etc are taken to be unanswerable and insignificant. But orthodox christianity agrees that while rationality and imagination cannot supply access to truth, rather than abandoning the search for truth, they should return to the Bible, to the church and tradition for the truth.

Consult also the article by Craig Bartholomew, 'Reading the Old Testament in Postmodern Times', *Tyndale* 49/1 (1998): 91–114 on recent proposals by Rendtorff, Brueggemann and Clines in reading the Old Testament in the light of postmodernism.

Chapter Three

Recent Approaches to Interpretation

Interpretation is the fuel that drives understanding. The making of meaning is what scripture is all about, the effort by every possible device to make sense of the divine in search of the human, and the human in search of the divine, the joy of discovery, the joy of the loss. If scripture is about anything in all of its splendid diversity, it is about this, and so it is not really about whether there is or not interpretation in the reading of scripture. The question is, what kind of interpretation?

(Gomes 1996:33)

3.1 Introduction

Several approaches have been developed to enable readers to interpret and understand biblical texts. Each of them has its own strengths and weaknesses. Nevertheless, the three most common approaches used in biblical interpretation are the author-oriented, text-oriented and reader-oriented models.

3.2 Author-Oriented

This approach focuses on the author's intention as a conduit for understanding the meaning in the text.[1] He is seen as a skilful agent painstakingly crafting his text. Since there is a conscious intention in writing his text, attention is paid to his feelings, experiences, state of mind etc. Ultimately, he controls the meaning of the text.[2]

The words in a text are expressions of his intention and state of mind. To understand the text, we need to understand the author. The text supplies bibliographical information so that meaning may be determined. What the author intended to mean, is what the text means. Thus the locus of meaning resides in the author's intention.

The role of the interpreter is passive and his task is simply to discover and confirm the author's state of mind as well as his intended communique. Author centred approach seeks to get *behind* the text. Its textual meaning is determined by its origin which has given rise to author-intention, historical context and tracing of Ur-text and original readers' expectation (Juhl 1980:47).[3]

3.2.1 Evaluation

One of the strengths of this approach is that it takes the author seriously by respecting his "rights" in the final determiner of meaning. An author centred approach does not seek to subvert the author's intention. It makes a lot of sense that the author would attempt to communicate his meaning through a text since his primary aim is to address an audience. Hence the more we know of the author's biographical data such as background, his make up, etc., the more successful we will be in understanding his words.

One major criticism that has been directed against this approach is the anonymity of the author. We do not know who that writer is. Anonymity in writing is not uncommon in the Bible. Many of the biblical writers were anonymous except for Ezra and Nehemiah and some New Testament writers. Speaking of the Old Testament writers, Sternberg (1985:64) quips that 'the sad truth is that we know practically nothing about biblical writers—even less than about the processes of writing and transmission—and it looks as though they never will.' Therefore, it is a grave mistake to suggest that one cannot understand the writing of the author without understanding or knowing who that person is.[4] The screw of interpretation will have to be unturned when it is discovered that the author whom we thought to be the writer turns out to be somebody else.

Another criticism is that 'complete authorial meaning is unobtainable because it is the product of the author's individual consciousness' (Jeanrond 1982:4), therefore to probe for meaning in the mind of the author is illusory. Since the author is dead, an imaginative quantum leap is needed to surmise his beliefs and knowledge as well as his intention.

As Robinson (1988:95) perceptively hints out

> Focusing on the author's life subordinates the meaning of the text to the task of understanding the author, destroying the integrity of structural patterns within the text by referring them to external impulses in the mind of the author. On the other hand, maintaining the autonomy of the textual meaning removes the warrant for direct inferences about the author's person.

We need to bear in mind that biblical texts could have undergone several redaction and editorial changes. They might have passed through several editions before reaching the public and what the author originally wrote could be changed for economic, censorship, political and cultural reasons.

Pseudonomy has also been asserted that the author could have purposefully constructed an implied author in the text who may be speaking instead of the actual author. There seems to be no criteria whereby an author's intention can be judged.

According to the critics, those who adopt this approach are guilty of what Wimsatt and Beardsley (1946) call *intentional fallacy* which makes an unwarranted switch from concentration of the poem (text) to a visionary leap of the author's mindset. Wimsatt asserts that in most instances, the poet's intentions are irretrievable; interest ought to be on how a poem works rather than what was intended; once a poem is published it becomes a public property rather than private because language is social rather than personal. The broad implication is that meaning can still be discovered by using the right linguistic tools and that while an author may not always be trusted, we can always trust his work.

As Wellek and Warren (1973:42) perceive:

> The whole idea that the *intention* of the author is the proper subject of literary history seems, however quite mistaken. The meaning of a work of art is not exhausted by, or even equivalent to, its intention. As a system of values, it leads an independent life.

Another criticism is the failure of this approach to see that the texts have a public existence, independent of the author. From the post-structuralist's viewpoint, 'To give a text to an author is to impose a limit on the text, to furnish it with a final signified, to close the writing' (Barthes 1977:147). We should not impose an author on the text because by so doing we are imposing 'an archaic monism on a brave new pluralistic world' (Burke 1992:24). Furthermore, 'a text is not a line of words releasing a single theological meaning but a multi dimensional space in which a variety of writings, none of them original, blend and clash' (Barthes 1977:146).

As Burke (1992:22) observes,

> . . .the death of the author is the first step to refusing to assign an ultimate meaning to the text and like the death of God in the nineteen century, both deaths attest to a departure of belief in authority, presence, intention, omniscience and creativity.[5]

3.3 Text-Oriented

The primacy of the text is the thrust of this approach. Textual features such as artistry, stylistic devices, figures of speech, compositional techniques, etc. are taken as a guide to meaning and solving knotty problems. This approach assumes that a text is organised around a structure and that the layout and language used direct the reader to specific meaning.

Such an approach argues for a deliberate break between the author and the text. When that happens, 'a text is freed from its putative referential obligations, and language becomes the primary point of departure because texts belong to language and not to the author (Burke 1992:43). And, because the death of the author results in the texts becoming a 'jouissant affirmation of indeterminacy, a dance of the pen, a Dionysian threshing floor' (ibid:24). However, since the text is a work of somebody,[6] it treats the text with reverence and interprets it responsibly and aesthetically. As Steiner (1989:4) declares 'the conjecture is that "God" is not because our grammar is outworn; but that grammar lives and generates worlds because there is the wager on God'.

This approach also seeks to balance both opposing views (Author & Reader oriented) by recognising the ancient and modern context. It does not seek to deny matters such as historical context and the author's intention. Neither is it concerned with the historical reconstruction of the author. It simply brackets them.

As Wilson (1993:16) writes,

> Every text is the work of an author. The author can, however, be considered as separate from the text, and we are concerned with the internal determinants of the text and therefore with the author as presented by the text itself.

A text-oriented approach also argues for the autonomy of the text and has a predetermined meaning which is of interest to the reader. It holds that the function of the interpreter is to examine and comment on the text. Meaning is seen as determinate and ontologically stable and the final arbiter of validity. It is the result of a logical operation which is defined in the text itself.

3.3.1 Evaluation

The strength of a text oriented approach is that it allows the text's truth claims as well as the textual world (imperfect as it is because of our limited perspective) to be taken seriously. Other strengths include the objective criteria by which the validity of an interpretation can be judged since the text has veto power; and the vicious circle of hermeneutics can be broken. It is consistent with the Christian understanding of the Canon where Scripture is taken to be *norma normans* and authoritative rather than a tradition behind Scripture.

Some of its criticisms include the failure to take account of the textual production and corruption; attempting to smuggle the author in through the back door; assuming meaning to be transcendent and universal; ignoring the fact that textual interpretation is affected by presuppositions and that interpretation differs according to different historical contexts and communities. All these factors influence and affect interpretation.

This approach has also been criticised on the grounds of too much independence and detachment from the author. Its slavish dependence on the literary artifacts and failing to recognise meaning is created by the reader.

From the post structuralist viewpoint, the textual approach is also criticised for *logocentrism* where there is an overemphasis of the word as well as inappropriate implication that all forms of thought are based on the desire for truth.

3.4 Reader-Oriented[7]

The centre of attention is on the reader[8] whose relationship to the text is dialectical and dynamic.[9] It is more interested in the process than the product. Meaning is not inherent in the text but emerges only as the reader enters into a dialogue with the text. Meaning lies in the adjustment and in the readers' revision and expectation. It does not come neatly packaged in the text.

A text has no existence like words on a page. Neither is there meaning in the text except potentially. Meaning is subjective and is not embedded in the text but is the result of an interaction between the reader and the text. It only takes an existence when it is read by the reader. In that process, the text becomes an open system of signs that forces the reader to complete its meaning. Therefore, the reader needs to participate actively to generate (mediate) meaning in the text. The reader is the text's true producers. As an active agent, he recreates meaning and completes its meaning by reading.

Roland Barthes sees text as 'a multi-dimensional space in which are married and contested several writings, none of which is original; the text is a fabric of quotations, resulting from a thousand sources of culture' (1968:53). Multiple reading/meaning of a text is made possible because of the complex codes in the text. Reading produces pleasures and ecstatic bliss because the text is open ended. By traversing through the various textual codes, they induce the thrill of losing oneself in the text and finding oneself elsewhere.

Reader oriented approach highlights the reading encounter. It is a shift from a static objective meaning bound in a text to a more subjective meaning. It sees meaning not as ready made, buried in the ground, waiting to be dug up but generated by readers. Instead of what determines meaning, it is who determines reading; it moves from what does a text says to what does a text do. Logical rules used are functional in concept. The preferred vocabulary is 'interpretive aims' rather than 'textual meaning'.

A reader-oriented interpretation looks for textual clues to tell them what particular set of rules to activate in reading a text. The dictum of Alberto Caeiro is true: *The only meaning inherent in things is that there is no meaning inherent in things.* In other words,

> Text is no longer regarded as possessing objective, inherent pattern of meaning. Meaning is now envisioned as a function or a relation between the text and the reader's code which it is confronted. Text is merely a set of potentialities for sense making by the reader at all levels.
>
> (Valdes 1978:180)

Objectivity is not possible because all readers read from different perspectives. Therefore, meaning is not discovered but generated (created) through coding and decoding the text. The same word may yield different meanings because of different interpretive contexts. The text is open ended with meaning being indeterminate and pluralistic. Texts are not regarded as closed systems but a two way traffic; neither do they determine meaning but the reader. Ultimately, no reading is innocent because all reading is misreading, ideologically motivated and theologically laden. To put it in another way, meaning is in the eye of the beholder. As Leitch (1983:50) writes, 'this approach says there are no correct or objective readings only less or more energetic, interesting, careful or pleasurable misreading.' Eagleton (1983:721) adds 'the text merely serves as cues to the reader with an invitation to constitute a piece of language into meaning.'

Ultimately, texts can be used in whatever way readers like because 'like dead men and women, [they] have no rights, no aims, no interests' (Morgan and Barton 1989:7).

3.4.1 Evaluation

The strength of this approach is that it helps readers to read with great awareness of what they are doing as they read thereby leading to greater responsibility in reading. This approach has no one particular or predominant philosophical Archimedean point. It also values sensitivity in response and a direct personal encounter which in turn will recreate the text in new form in the reader's own experience.

Readers are invited to approach the text creatively. Its attempt to free the reader from the text and from its past moorings in order to emphasise the presentness of the text appears commendable but not without a heavy price to pay. As Roland Barthes (1968:53–55) has pointed out, once we remove the author, our claim to decipher a text becomes quite useless and what we have then is the birth of the reader at the cost of the death of the Author. The author's[10] death culminates in the deregulation of interpretation and a reader's reading becomes as authoritative and creative as the original. Meyer (1991:10) criticises the reader-oriented approach because it 'often gave the contrary impression of an excess of readings that outdid its complexity and creativity the text being read.'

The right of the interpreter to use (misuse?) the texts has profound ramifications as pointed out by Vanhoozer. First, it is the present context of the reader and not the historical context of the text that is important. Second, the determinative factor for good interpretation is dependent on the reader's interpretive aims. Because texts can be used in whatever the reader chooses. Hence, the text 'becomes wishing well where readers draw up what they like.' Third, since there are no norms there can be no misinterpretation. If there is no misinterpretation, there can be no one correct meaning. Any single meaning is correct because meaning is generated by readers.

Other criticisms highlighted by McKnight (1993:213–214) are that such an approach is not comprehensive enough; it may be inappropriate due to its literary orientation; a likely suspect because it stems from fictional literature; its lack of attention to the author's intention and its unsettling character. Since it has no textual or contextual constraints, interpreters can cast off restraints which may eventually lead to hermeneutical anarchy and nihilism. As Steiner (1989:57) retorts: 'The unarrested infinity of conceivable propositions and statements entails the logic of nullity and of nihilism'. The logical outcome of reader-oriented approach is, if something can mean anything, it will eventually become nothing! The idea of anything goes is the result of the "cancer of uncontrolled interpretation". Eco's (1992:151) allegation is correct: 'When everybody is right, everybody is wrong and I have the right to disregard everybody's point of view.'

As Ricoeur writes, '. . . a text is a finite space of interpretation; there is not just one interpretation, but, on the other hand, there is not an infinite number of them.'[11] Finally, 'If we substitute the authority of the reader for that of the text, we cannot help but commit interpretive violence against the text', opines Vanhoozer (1995b:14). We need to be reminded that 'texts have an independent existence over and against the interpreter' (Noble 1995:1).

This approach is guilty of what Wimsatt and Beardsley (1946) call *affective fallacy* which concentrates on the emotional response at the expense of the textual words. Such concern deflects attention on the organisation of the text and whatever associations generated will be idiosyncratic responses and reactions. Metaphorically speaking, 'they have taken the Lord out of the tomb, and we do not know where they have laid him'.

Although its pluralistic perspective is its strength, its lack of control is its weakness. This approach has lots of subjectivism and there is a lack of control in reading the text. It opens the floodgates of unrestrained subjectivity. There is a tendency to resist any kind of methodology that is correct. Inevitably, 'once textual critics ruthlessly banish the author as the primary determiner of textual meaning, no principle remains to establish interpretation validity,' echoes Henry (1979:314).

As the reader is the active agent in making the text speaks, the author loses control of meaning and recedes to the background (Conrad 199:1). Because readers are not constrained by literary dynamics and authorial intention, they can generate an unlimited plurality of meanings and without any safeguards which can lead to hermeneutical *tohu wabohu*. As Wright (1992:59) correctly observes that in the final analysis 'the only thing to do with a text is to play with it for oneself: I must see what it does to me, and not ask whether there is another mind out there behind the text. . .There will be no right or wrong reading; only my reading and your reading.' Ultimately, by seeking to free the reader from the slavery to the text, advocates of reader-oriented model are exchanging one problematic model for another.

Belsey (1980:29) summarises it best when she remarks,

> At its best, interest in the reader is entirely liberating, a rejection of authorial tyranny in favour of the participation of readers in the production of a plurality of meanings: at its worst, reader-theory merely constructs a new authority figure as guarantor of a single meaning, a timeless transcendent, highly trained model reader who cannot be wrong.

Finally, Vanhoozer's perceptive assessment is correct when he says that since there are no criteria to judge false readings, the texts can be manipulated to mean whatever we wish. On that score anything can be justified including acts of murder, robbery, suicide and genocide![12]

3.5 Deconstructionism[13]

The point of departure for describing deconstructionism is poststructuralism which is an (over) reaction against structuralism. A brief description of structuralism is helpful for understanding deconstructionism. Structuralism argues for objective meaning in structures. In essence, it sees texts as system of signs that need decoding in order to discover meaning in the text. The task of the reader is to chart the basic narrative unit and determine the structural configuration beneath those surface codes.

Structuralism operates on the premise that all languages have a set of structured relationships which possess meaning. It further theorises that cultures develop literary documents (texts) which provide structures of meaning where people can make sense out of their experiences. Meanings can be discovered by studying the network of relationships in the text. Structuralism rejects the epistemology of the new hermeneutic (all interpretations are subjective) and accepts that presuppositions can be neutralised by suspending judgement of meaning.[14]

Poststructuralism (deconstructionism) was popularised by Jacques Derrida in the 60's and rose to prominence in the 70's. He is considered to be the father of deconstructionism which is influenced by Nietzsche and Heideggerian philosophy. It is heavily weighted towards language and postulates that the key to understanding social organisation, social meanings, power and individual consciousness is through language. According to Goosen (1996:384), 'deconstructionism is an assembly of provocative practices, anarchistic strategies or nomadic tactics, all set not only to undermine the idea of an all inclusive identity, but also to open new vistas for the ever evasive and inappropriable other.'[15]

A deconstructionist considers language to be slippery yet resourceful which refuses to be limited by what the writer says. There is always an unpredictable and uncontrollable meaning that seems to simmer in the text waiting to explode. There is no *presence* of meaning in the text but only *difference* and *absence*. Its presupposition is a non foundationalism which claims we do not have a clear and certain way of knowing things by which we can build upon knowledge and values. The focus of deconstructionism is not on the cognitive dimensions of communication but on stories, metaphors, and symbols that give continuity to the human family.

Vanhoozer's point is well taken when he opines

> deconstructive reading mercilessly exposes the reader's interests by undoing interpretation and by exposing the rhetoric, not logic, behind it. Deconstruction detoxifies the poisoned well. It is the ever vigilant attempt to prevent the act of reading to come to rest in a settled interpretation, for the makings of many meanings there is no end.

Philosophically, deconstructionism takes a very sceptical approach in reading a text concerning the possibility of finding any coherent/single

meaning or stable elements in language. It seeks to undo a text by expos-
ing reading as functions of various ideological forces. Every structure of
the text like language is arbitrary and conventional. By so doing it seeks to
deconstruct the accumulation of power in interpretation. According to
(Hawthorn 1994:108),

> . . .[It] aims at showing the inherent contradictions and paradoxes in logocentric
> approaches that emphasises on a word centred view of literature where the cen-
> tre underwrites and fixes linguistic meaning but is itself beyond scrutiny or chal-
> lenge.

Deconstructionism seeks to reveal the illusory status of the centre and
challenges all claims to textual coherence, unified meaning, order or unit
by trying to do away with traditional concepts, subject them to fragmentation through the principle of differance.
    According to van Wolde (1994:1970),

> This deconstructionism is marked by oppositional thinking:the constraints of the
> author's intention is replaced by absolute freedom, the text with a single meaning
> is replaced by a text with an infinite number of meanings, the unique importance
> of the text for the meaning is replaced by the unique importance of the reader for
> the meaning, the determination of the meaning by the social language code is
> replaced by the individual giving of meaning.

It also challenges the modern assumption that the human being is a rational and coherent subject. It sees human reasoning and subjectivity as a by
product of social forces and language because who we are, is constructed
by the way reality is named to us. In other words, human subjectivity is
constructed by language which is not fixed but built as words acquire
meanings in specific historical situations which are always the site of competing meaning and therefore there is struggle (Vanhoozer).
    Deconstruction does not mean to destroy but to undo a text. To
deconstruct the text is to see incoherence in the text and to subvert truths.
A deconstructive reading is a reading which 'analyses the specificity of a
text's critical difference from itself' and assumes that 'every text's structure ultimately deconstructs, yielding not a single determinate meaning
but a potentially infinite variety of meanings' (Keegan 1995:2).
    Since there is nothing beyond the text, everything starts from inside.
Quite often it questions some seemingly unimportant item like a word,
letter, a phrase, title in order to break down a concept or a passage in the
text. Part of its purpose is as Derrida (1976:158) claims to prevent interpreters from the

> . . . repression of limits and tradition so that fresh interpretation can take place. Significant reading is not so much a reproduction, a reactualisation of meaning that is explained by authors or resident in the text. But reading that challenges the reader through opening his world to creative discovery to new anomalies that may be suggested as much irrational (eagle/beagle, hear/here, etc).

Since conclusion connotes control and direction and distorts the nature of texts, there can be no final conclusion (deconstructing reading). Every deconstruction opens itself for further deconstruction.

3.5.1 Evaluation

Hunter (1987:136–138) has highlighted the positive features of deconstructionism such as viewing the text from a different angle and contributing to finding (new?) meaning in the Biblical texts. Whether it contributes to confusion or clarification of the text, it helps to reach more clarity. Deconstructionism urges 'a serious approach to the text itself and its characters who are all part of textuality and not realities outside the texts' (ibid:137).

Another positive contribution deconstuctionism makes is in intertextuality. It is asserted that Biblical texts were constantly rewritten and reused. Therefore, it is difficult to distinguish the original texts from those redacted. Instead of trying to establish the fixed form and interpreting them irrespective of their contexts, deconstructionism suggests that whenever a new text is written (re-texted) it should be interpreted in its originality. In other words, the bedrock qualifications for pursuing biblical studies are semitic languages (Hayman 1995:443) rather than Derrida's French.[16]

On the other hand, deconstruction as a hermeneutical tool has been sharply criticised on several fronts. We summarise the criticisms of Hunter (1987:134–135) who argues that no matter how much texts are deconstructed, they still communicate! In other words, if we accept the idea of contradictions and paradoxes, why do we still understand meaning from the text? If communication is possible, there must be meaning and if meaning is understood, there must be denotation although in differences.

Moreover, to separate speech from writing is a false dichotomy because there can be no writing without thinking nor denotation. Whenever texts are produced, writers either consciously used/contemplated structures or consciously ignored structures. Since that is the case, the notion of structure should not be ignored in hermeneutics. By deconstructing to understand the texts better, deconstructionists are imposing a different way of interpretation on texts than that created in the western metaphysical tradition. 'If deconstructionists' are afraid of meaning, it is not worth much in the interpretational business other than being a critical position and a hypocritical style of accusation,' (Hunter ibid:135).

Another criticism is its use of jargons such as spacing, interability, ecriture, undecidables, taxeme, etc. All these make writings appear esoteric when they are not in actual fact.

Leitch (1983:253) criticises the deconstructionist 'as a peculiar connoiseur who stops at the unimportant, gazes emotionally at its surface, and let exaggerated wonder become everything.' Steiner (1986:115) goes a step further by saying that 'the often repulsive jargon, to the contrived obscurantism and specious pretension to technicality which makes the bulk of post-structuralist and deconstructive theory and practice, particularly among its academic epigones, unreadable'.

Henry (1995:39) hits the nail on the head when he argues that

> Deconstructionism strips reality and written texts of inherent meaning. It reduces language to but a social construct mirroring the interpreter's personal perspective. Consequently, every interpreter is free to handle the text selectively, that is, to deconstruct it, and to refashion favoured segments into fresh readings that reflect one's preferences without evident anchorage in the text.

From the standpoint of biblical exegesis, deconstructionism is problematic because it gives unrestrained freedom to the reader but accords the biblical text a minimal role. Inevitably, the ethical and communicative functions of the text are denied. In the arena of textual meaning 'a text may possess so many different meanings that it cannot have a meaning' (Cuddon 1992:222–225). Since it stops short of having a particular meaning in a text, it is guilty of committing a 'hermeneutical coitus interruptus' (Newton).

In the final analysis, deconstructionism eliminates God, freedom, purposive agency, self, realism, truth, good and evil and historical meaning (Vanhoozer).

3.5.2 Hermeneutical Implications

What are some of the implications of deconstructionism? Part of its implications implies that there is no longer a unifying centre or the basis of meaning. It views the Bible 'as reifying and ratifying the status quo that provides warrant for the subjugation of women, justifying colonialism and enslavement, rationalizing homophobia and legitimizing the power of hegemonic classes of people' (Postmodernist Bible 1995:4).

It sees no basis to distinguish one perspective as better than the others and consequently there is no truth to know. There is nothing that grounds the structure of signification. Every sign is an interpretation of other interpretations. Its tenets consist of wordplay and word associations.

It rejects the dichotomy between the reader and the text. Truth is not to be found but to be constructed. What is true is what one believes to be true. Reality is not to be perceived but to be conceived. 'Since no objective truths exist all religion reflects a historically conditioned bias' (Henry 1995: 41). Therefore 'religion is marginalised and trivialised and has only private cognitive significance but irrelevant to external institutions, corporate life, and cultural expression' (ibid:41–42).

The reader is free to deconstruct the text from all the meaning of the author and its past understanding. By so doing the reader is at liberty to develop his 'own game on the playground of the text.' It uses a rhetorical approach where it sees no fixed norms or dogmas but only metaphorical. Since readers cannot reach a final interpretation of meaning, they bring their own interpretive rules on the text.

Hence, the unavoidable conclusion is that in interpreting a text, no one can arrive at complete or final meaning because 'the meaning of a text is always unfolding and unrolling just ahead of the interpreter like a never ending carpet whose final edge never reveals itself' (Hawthorn 1994:34). The epistemic premise of foundationalism which says knowledge consists of a set of beliefs is to be rejected. Absolute relativism prevails; objective truth is intolerable and non existent. Any transcendent centre of reality is disavowed. According to Payne & Habib (1990:6),

> In its modest form deconstruction seeks out breaks, slippages, contradictions vertiginous moments by which we are constituted. In radical form, it promotes the dissolution of meaning in order to bring down the power structure of the text.

This implies that a text can be read as saying something quite different from what it appears to be saying. The text may be read as carrying a plurality of significance. Or it may say many different things which are at odds or contradictory to and subversive of what may have been seen as a single, stable meaning.

Ultimately, the deconstructionists by rejecting 'the metaphysics of presence' behind any meaning and 'disolving meaning simply into a strategy for coping' (Wilkinson 1996:135) implies that there are no invalid interpretations, there can be no misinterpretation or misunderstanding of the texts.

Notes

1   A strong advocate of this position is Hirsch (1967) and for a strong defense of authorial intent, see N. T. Wright, *The New Testament and the People of God* (Minneapolis: Fortress, 1992):58–64 . Cf. the sober critique of Erickson (1993:11–32) and G. B. Madison, *The Hermeneutics of Postmodernity: Figures and Themes* (Bloomington: Indiana University Press, 1988) especially chapter 1.

2   Within the author centred approach there are two schools of thoughts concerning meaning. There is only one meaning in the text and the other a deeper meaning (*sensus plenior*) in the text. The finding of a deeper meaning in the text is possible since the 'Holy Spirit is the ultimate author of Scripture, meanings of the text unknown and unintended by the human authors are possible to discover through the continuing revelatory work of the Holy Spirit to believers in reading' (De Young and Hunty 1995:13).

It is beyond the scope of this monograph to critique the *sensus plenior* method except to say that while such an approach is commendable because it seeks to give a greater role to the work of the Holy Spirit and to personal application, it also muddies the hermeneutical waters. I maintain that making a distinction between *sense* and *significance* is a more viable solution to the hermeneutical puzzle. For a defence of the *sensus plenior* as well as a challenge against the 'single meaning' approach, see James De Young and Sarah Hunty, *Beyond the Obvious: Discover the deeper Meaning of Scripture* (Gresham, Oregon: Vision House, 1995) and William Sanford Lasor, 'The *Sensus Plenior* and Biblical Interpretation', in Donald K. Mckim (ed), *A Guide to Contemporary Hermeneutics* (Grand Rapids: Wm B. Eerdmans, 1986):47–64.

For a critique of *sensus plenior*, see Douglas J. Moo, 'The Problem of *Sensus Plenior*', in D. A. Carson and John D. Woodbridge (eds), *Hermeneutics, Authority and Canon* (England: Intervarsity Press, 1986).

3   By and large, it is fair to say that many advocates who take this position also support the 'grammatical-historical method' in exegesis. For a brief but good discussion of this method, see William B. Tolar, 'The Grammatical Historical method', in Bruce Corley, Steve Lemke and Grant Lovejoy (eds), *Biblical Hermeneutics: A Comprehensive Introduction to Interpreting Scripture* (Nashville: Tennessee, 1996):217–243.

4   A classic example that comes to my mind is the book of Hebrews in the New Testament. To the best of my knowledge no New Testament scholar has ever claimed that since we do not know who the author is, we are not able to understand the text.

5   Beardsley (1970) in his book, *The Possibility of Criticism* gives the following arguments against authorial intention (see especially pages 18–20; 30–31).

1) Some texts have been formed without the agency of the author; hence without authorial meaning, yet it has a meaning.

2) Meaning of a text can change after its author has died. But the author cannot change his meaning after he has died. Therefore textual meaning is not identical to authorial meaning.

3) A text can have meaning its author is not aware of.

4) Texts acquire meaning through the interaction of their words without the intervention of an authorial will.

5) Textual meaning is identical to the authorial meaning.

In a sense, the text is independent of the author because he is no longer present or controls it. The text has potential to transcend the author and dialogue with the author is not possible.

6   Normally when a text is considered in a textual analysis, it refers to "implied author". See Bonnycastle (1991:11).

7   The orientation for sections 3.3, 3.4 and 7.2 is taken from Vanhoozer's unpublished notes. Citations by Vanhoozer in this monograph is taken from those notes unless otherwise stated. The influence of his writings is readily acknowledged.

8   The reader centred approach (commonly known as reader response) represents diversity of thoughts. See Suleiman (1980:3–45) for details of six types of readers. McKnight (1993:197) observes that 'reader–response criticism is not a conceptually unified criticism; it is a spectrum of positions.'

     For distinctions between Reader response and Reception theory, see Robert C Holub, *Reception Theory: A Critical Introduction* (London & NY: Methuen, 1984) xii–xiii. See also, Michael Cahill, 'Reader-response Criticism and the Allegorizing Reader', *Theological Studies* 57:1 (1996):89–96.

9   Porter (1990:279) summarises the basic tenets of a Reader Response Approach.

1) The centre of authority is shifted from the text itself or author to the reader.

2) Readers are involved in a complex interplay with the text which chronicles his or her struggle to comprehend it.

3) Meaning is not a single thing—a propositional truth but readers making them responsible to the text. In other words, meaning of text is not inherent but produced or actualised.

4) Meaning produced as a result of interaction cannot be checked against any objective standard but is a product of reading strategy.

5) Those who hold to similar reading strategy constitute an interpretive community.

10   Traditionally speaking, the author is considered to be the owner of the text with authority over it as well as the final court of appeal for meaning.

11   Paul Ricoeur, 'World of Text, World of Reader', in Mario J. Valdes (ed), *A Ricoeur Reader: Reflection & Imagination* (New York: Harvester Wheatsheaf, 1991):494.

12   See the excellent critique by Paul R Noble on the value of Reader Response approach for use in Biblical Interpretation in 'Hermeneutics and Post-Modernism: Can we have a Radical Reader Response Theory? Part 1', in *Religious Studies* 31 (1994):419–436 and 'Hermeneutics and Post-Modernism: Can we have a Radical Reader Response Theory? Part II', in *Religious Studies* 31 (1995):1–22.

Noble concludes that the reader response theory as represented by Stanley Fish is unsound but a form of postmodernism that biblical studies should reject.There can be objective discussion about what is true, reader independent meaning of a text. We should not move towards the Fishian direction.

See also the critical evaluation of Readers Response by Norman R. Gulley,'Reader-Response Theories in Postmodern Hermeneutics: A Challenge to Evangelical Theology,' in David S. Dockery (ed), *The Challenge of Postmodernism: An Evangelical Engagement* (Wheaton, Illinois: Victor Books/ SP Publications, 1995):208–238.

13   A discussion of other spectrums of interpretive methodologies like feminist, liberation, materialist, psychoanalytic hermeneutics is beyond the scope of this monograph. Moreover, they deserve more discussion than this context can provide.

For a good introduction to the various methodologies, see the excellent series of articles in Leander E. Keck, Thomas Long, et al. (eds), *The New Interpreters' Bible* (Nashville: Abingdon, 1994) as well as Gerald Bray, *Biblical Interpretation: Past and Present* (Downers Grove, Illinois: Intervarsity Press, 1996) especially pages 461–488.

For Feminists' orientation, see Maggie Hum, *A Reader's Guide to Contemporary Feminist Literary Criticism* (Hertfordshire: Harvester Wheatsheaf,1994) and David Rutledge, Reading marginally: *Feminism, Deconstructionism and the Bible* (Leiden: Brill; Biblical Interpretation series 21; 1996); Athalya Brenner and Carole Fontaine, *A Feminist Companion to Reading the Bible: Approaches, Methods and Strategies* (England: Sheffield) Emily Cheney, *She Can Read: Feminist Reading Strategies for Biblical Narrative* (Valley Forge, Pennslyvania: Trinity Press International, 1996); J. D. H. Amador, 'Feminist Biblical Hermeneutics: A Failure of Theoretical Nerve', *Journal of the American Academy of Religion* 66/1 (1998): 39–57 and J. C. Anderson, 'Mapping Feminist Biblical Criticism', *Critical Review of Books in Religion* 2 (1991): 21–44.

14   Some criticisms that have been aimed at structuralism include a lack of a strong philosophical foundation, an overemphasis of codes and binaries, a tendency to major on the minors, and lopsided in its emphasis on deep structures.

15   Goosen (1996:384–385) puts the differences between deconstructionism and postmodernism this way:

While deconstructionism tends to emphasize an inerasable lack of meaning in every attempt to construct the world, postmodernism tends to emphasize an over-supply of meaningful answers. While deconstructionism therefore often renders us speechless and even hapless while confronting us with a definite lack of meaning, postmodernism tends to empower us with as many answers as we would like to have in any given situation.

16   For a positive approach to deconstructionism, see Simon Critchley, *The Ethics of Deconstructionism: Derrida and Levinas* (Oxford: Blackwell, 1992).

For the most up to date overview of recent criticism, see Elizabeth A. Castelli, Stephen D. Moore (eds), et al., *The Postmodern Bible: The Bible and Culture Collective* (New Haven: Yale University Press, 1995).

For other critiques, see Aystradur Eysteinsson, *The Concept of Modernism* (Ithaca: Cornell University, Press 1990); John Mcgowan, *Postmodernism and its Critics* (Ithaca: Cornell University Press, 1991); Christopher Norris, *What's Wrong with Postmodernism?* (Baltimore: Johns Hopkins University Press, 1990); ibid, *The Truth about Postmodernism* (Oxford: Blackwell Publishers, 1993) and ibid, *Against Relation: Philosophy of Science, Deconstruction and Critical Theory* (Oxford: Blackwell Publishers, 1997).

Chapter Four

Toward a Final Form Text

To work with the final form of the texts, removed from the diachronic framework and envisaged now as relatively autonomous linguistic artefacts, is therefore to propose a major reorientation or paradigm-shift within the discipline. (Watson 1994:15)

4.1 The Rise of Biblical Criticism[1]

The beginning of the Enlightenment (Aufklärung) in the eighteenth century is considered by many to be an intellectual watershed because it defines a new and different way of thinking in all aspects of life.[2] Enlightenment (also called the age of Reason) is 'man's release from his self-incurred tutelage' (Kant 1784).[3]

According to Inwood (1995:236), some of the common tenets of Enlightenment include the following:

1) Reason is man's central capacity which enables him to think and act correctly.
2) By nature, Man is good.
3) Individuals and humanity can progress towards perfection.
4) Since all human beings are equal in rationality, they should all be granted equality before the law and individual liberty.
5) Tolerance is to be granted to all other creeds and different way of life.
6) Beliefs are to be accepted on the basis of reason and not ecclesiastical authority, tradition or sacred texts.
7) The non rational aspects of human nature is down played and anything (eg customs, etc), which is the result of historical peculiarities rather than the exercise of reason, is to be devalued.

Broadly speaking, human reason not only became autonomous but it also reigned supreme in the Enlightenment period. The courage to use reason (Kant), the freeing up of the human spirit to question everything including the Bible and freedom from the shackles of religious authority and ecclesiastical traditions summarise what the Enlightenment period is all about.[4]

Inevitably, science and religion collided resulting in the collapse of faith and the decentering of the bible. The consequences for religion were far reaching.

Historical criticism became the major interpretive paradigm in the mid nineteenth and early twentieth centuries. 'Historical criticism is reflective of a certain set of epistemological assumptions that go under the general terms *objective, scientific* and *positivistic*' (Brueggemann 1997:103; emphasis his). Historical criticism interprets the Bible through historical but critical framework. The Bible was studied scientifically/critically rather than devotionally.

Historical critical reconstruction of biblical texts became very important because of several assumptions: One, Scripture is understood as a historical narrative unfolding the story of Israel, the church as well as the salvation story. Two, there are errors, contradictions and inconsistencies of details in the text. Three, there is an official version of the story it tells (history in the text); an unofficial version of the story it bears witness to (history behind the text) and the story of its origin, formation and development (history of the text).[5] Four, there is not one story but several (and at times similar) stories told from different theological perspectives. Hence, different methodologies were invented and used in reconstructing history. Part of its reconstructive effort includes analysis, dissecting and subdividing of biblical writings into sources, and chronological rearrangement of the books in the Bible.

Texts were seen as historical artifacts for reconstruction of critical history. They cannot be taken at face value and must be critiqued and reinterpreted.

The result was that divine inspiration, divine revelation, truth claims, reliability and uniqueness of the bible, biblical accuracy and ecclesiastical authority were all greatly challenged and undermined. The claim for divine authorship was either rejected or modified as the role of individuals and communities were given prominence. Put simply, the status and symbol of the Bible was demoted.

Hence, in the light of these assumptions it is difficult if not impossible to maintain Scripture as the word of God. Scripture is no longer seen as 'a single fibre but a rope of many strands of different sizes woven together.' Therefore, the unity of Scripture is subverted and diversity is embraced. The locus of revelation is located outside the texts. The role of the human is (over) emphasised at the expense of the divine authorship.

Hermeneutically speaking, the Bible was investigated scientifically with the interpreter becoming a historian asking questions pertaining to the date, place, audience, political, and religious circumstances. In the end, to put it metaphorically, 'the Ark of Scripture had fallen into the hands of the Philistines of the Enlightenment, who honoured man and reason above all things' (Mackie 1969:43).

4.2 The Inadequacy of Historical Criticism[6]

The historical method has been used for some two centuries in biblical studies. It has made some positive contributions to the entire enterprise of hermeneutics. According to Zeisler (1994:270–271), a historical critical approach to interpretation is right because Christianity (as well as Judaism) is a historical religion and the Bible is committed to history in that it contains an important element called *Heilsgeschichte* (history of God's saving act).

Another positive element of historical criticism is that it has helped interpreters to anchor the text in its historical context. To put it another way, the historical critics have a high 'respect for the integrity of the texts in their particularity' (Zeisler 1994:274). It seeks to ask what the text meant to the original audience. By insisting on the historical context as the perimeter for interpretation, the historical critics help to ensure that interpretation does not run wild. Moreover, it was a good safeguard mechanism against the excessive tendencies of earlier interpreters who used the allegorical method to interpret the texts (Stanton 1977:70). This to an extent prevents the texts from becoming exploited. It is not surprising that 'historical criticism gained some of its impetus as a protest against ecclesiastical traditions which were suspected of reading into the Bible what they wanted to find there' (Zeisler 1994:271).

Another of its strength lies in its commitment to philological and historical research while its intention is also commendable because it seeks to capture the import of the context and its true textual meaning.[7]

However, the weaknesses of historical criticism become more apparent as newer methodologies surface. Some of the weaknesses of historical criticism include alienation from other methods (Meyer 1991:3); its method leads to 'theological impoverishment' (Watson 1993:7) because it ignores the theological dimension of the text; failure to bridge the ancient text to modern context; inability to provide narrative direction and sepa-

rate texts and its meaning from that life' (McKnight 1993:103); inability
to see the big picture (ie, one can 'see fern seed but cannot see an elephant ten yards away in broad daylight' to use Lewis' famous phrase)
and 'the loss of innocence in literal reading' (Noll 1993:138).[8] Meyer
(1991:10) incisively comments that the historical approach 'often left an
impression of banality—monophonic interpretation of polyphonic texts'.
Rendtorff's (1998:42) assessment of historical criticism is that it is mainly
a negative method because 'it denies certain aspects of biblical texts that
up to then had been self evident', and 'the starting point . . . is the
suspicion that the text itself had no integrity'. Additionally, 'it has a dis-
tancing effect and makes the Bible appear to be strange, antique object to
be dissected rather than a Word to be heard and obeyed' (Pinnock
1984:144).

Historical criticism (more often than not hypercriticism with no pun
intended) according to Brueggemann (1997:104), is problematic because
as a method it became an end in itself rather than a means to an end.
That is to say 'criticism had become an end in itself, 'criticism understood
now as debunking suspicion and scepticism, and not in the service of
interpretation'. Because of its tendency to explain away 'any witness to
the text to the mysterious workings of God', and to rule out 'the primal
Subject of the text', such an approach not only 'misses the primary intentionality of the text', but is also 'incongruent with the text' (ibid). What is
left for the historical critics is philological commentary.

More often than not, the historical critics have a predilection to emend
the text as they think it ought to be rather than explaining the text as it is.
This is compounded by the dogmatic stance to see all parallel passages as
doublets rather than entertaining the possibility that they may be type
scenes, typologies or narrative analogies.[9] Rightly or wrongly, they have
been accused of 'parallelomania'.[10] As a result, many times they are right
in what they assert (ie sources have been used) but wrong in what they
have denied (eg, unity in diversity).

Its critics also claim that the atomistic method in biblical studies have
not produced fruitful results. Its starting point is off target because instead
of beginning from the 'known to the unknown' so that there will an an-
chorage on the text, it reverses the direction by starting from the 'unknown to the known'.

Another criticism is that it has a tendency to leave the extant text
quickly in order to go backwards to reconstruct its original text that it fails
to return to the given text (Rendtorff 1994:4). Moreover, the historical
critic's ability to tear ruthlessly apart a text is matched equally by his

inability to put the text back again.[11] In the end, as a method 'it has failed to deliver satisfactory and universally agreed results (Zeisler 1994:272).[12]

The adverse impact of historical criticism is that the Bible became a historical momento as the gap between scholars and laity widened; the relevance of scripture for modern people was subverted, the unity of biblical narrative was torpedoed through minute dissection as scholars replace ecclesiastical leadership as the final court of appeal for meaning.

> It is now clear to everybody that the historical-critical approach, however valuable, is woefully insufficient. It alone will not put us in touch with the underlying mystery; it alone will not bring us to those eternal realities towards the scriptures point; it alone will not enrich our lives with mysticism.[13]

While there may be some value in historical criticism,[14] there are many inadequacies that many see literary studies as a means as a viable alternative to regain the loss of innocence.[15]

4.3 Two Stellar Figures

Two of the well known luminaries that have emblazoned the biblical and literary stratosphere by challenging the hegemony of historical criticism are Frei (1994) and Childs (1979).[16] I summarise their insightful observations with implications for hermeneutics.

4.3.1 Hans Frei

He points out that during the precritical period the Bible was read literally and historically. Meaning can be found within the text. However, with the ascendancy of historical criticism, Frei argues a paradigm shift occurred in the latter half of the eighteen century which attempts to locate meaning not in the text but in the actual historical event. This resulted in *the eclipse of biblical narrative.*

Truth became equated with the historicity of the events outside the text. Hence, meaning was obtained by reference to things outside the narrative text. Therefore, 'truth' (or 'reality') of biblical narratives could only be affirmed if it fitted within the frame of reconstructed history. To put it in another way, a story is deemed to be 'untrue' if there is no reference to real events outside the text.

Moreover, the unified narrative of a sequential single story becomes undermined and disjointed because of the historical critics' predilection for dissection and analysis of sources.

As there was no direct continuity between the real events in the Bible and real events in later history, what was historically false could be theologically true. One profound consequence is that a distance was created between the narrative world (the literal meaning of biblical story) and the real historical world (reference to actual events). This results in a dichotomy between meaning and reference (ie, what the story says and what it is about). Therefore religious truth could/should be detached from the story itself, biblical theology and historical criticism became two different types of enterprises.

The solution Frei proposes is that biblical narratives should be treated on their own terms because they are autonomous. This means that the point of reference should not be reality nor the historicity of events. Neither should the meaning of the story (what the story says) be separated from its form (narrative structure or sequence of the story).[17]

4.3.2 Brevard Childs

According to Childs' assessment, historical critical method is theologically deficient because it has failed (refused?) to recognise the canonical form of the text which is given authority and normative value by the community by faith.

The historical critics have operated on the wrong assumption that texts are mainly to be treated as ancient documents containing information about the history of the Israelite religion. Hence the need for historical reconstruction and the development of traditions within the biblical material which at best is uncertain. Had the later believing communities operated on the premise of the historical critics, they would have considered Scripture non authoritative and could not move to theological appropriation because the texts are locked in the past.

To put it in another way, historical critics are asking questions from the texts which have not been designed to give them answers to their questions. Hence, the interpretive efforts of historical criticism are not appropriate nor effective for theological hermeneutics.

Childs' thesis is that the primary context for doing hermeneutics should be the canon[18] and not history. The reason is that the canon is the 'arena where the struggle for understanding takes place' (Childs 1985:15). There are two important aspects of the canon: historical and theological. Historically, this canonical process involved the slow development of texts and traditions, beginning in the early preexilic period and ending during the Hellenistic period.[19] Theologically, the formation of the canon is a process of reflection of certain sacred writings which has impacted on the community of faith. Hence we should recognise the Old Testament as an

authoritative and normative Scripture because the texts were intentionally shaped by communities of faith for present and future generations.

A canonical approach to interpreting the texts would begin with the
final form of the text rather than the reconstruction of the historical stages
of a book's development.[20] Second, the interpreter should seek to attempt to understand the particular shape and function of individual books
in the Hebrew canon.

Third, there is a need to read texts with reference to other texts (using
Scripture to interpret Scripture commonly known as "intertextuality") for
illumination because of their networking and interconnectivity.

Fourth, the theological witness of the text cannot be heard apart from
the voices of the communities of the faith who have shaped and inter-
acted with the canon in its long development.[21]

4.3.2.1 Implications of Old Testament as Scripture

There are several implications for Childs. One, the Old Testament is not
replaced by the appearance of the New Testament. The early Church
continued to value the Old Testament as Scripture even after the close of
the New Testament canon.[22] As Scripture is [contains] the Word of God,
it is normative and authoritative for the past, present and future community of believers.

Second, the Old Testament is a legitimate and revelatory part of Christian Scripture. It should be placed alongside the New Testament. It is the
word that is within the canonical text that is revelatory, not the particularities of the historical and social circumstances even though they might
have exerted influence on authors, tradents, and editors.

Third, the formulation of the tradition consisting of collection and ordering of the experiences of the divine, enable the canonisers to address
authoritatively future generations. Since the Old Testament is normative,
it is a collection of texts that is intrinsically theological.

Fourth, the Bible is not simply a collection of books filled with historical information to be used primarily for historical reconstruction by
historians.

Fifth, the canonical approach sees the biblical texts as primarily theological in nature. Therefore, the locus of authority is found in the biblical
texts because they are product of believing communities. Though there
are several prevailing voices in the texts, there is also an emerging predominant voice.

Finally, even critics must concede that the arrangement of biblical books
in a certain order and the restriction of the books to the present list,
Jewish and Christian were imposing certain hermeneutical constraints

upon the text. In other words, the canon serves as constraints and restraints for speculative reading.

4.3.2.2 Evaluation
As a start, for terminological exactitude, Childs prefers the term canonical approach rather than canonical criticism.[23]

The strength of Childs' approach is that the shaping of the canonical texts was intended to transcend their historical contexts and social history in order to speak God's Word to future communities. Hence, the past is connected to the present and the future thereby giving Scripture relevance.

Theological legitimacy is given to later redactors and bearers of tradition who attempted recontextualisation of an earlier message for a new setting. Hence, the established axiom of the historical critics that the earliest stage of a tradition is "authentic" and normative, while later stages are "inauthentic" less historical, no longer holds water. As Ratzinger (1994:52) correctly notes 'this canonical approach is a right reaction against placing an exaggerated value on what is supposed to be original and early, as if this alone were authentic'. Moreover, this approach does not see the need for philosophical or other theological systems for validation.

Its interest in what the text means rather than meant is commendable; to say a text's theological significance for the church is not to be located in the original meaning but rather in the church's continuing use of the text.

It takes the canonical context of biblical writings very seriously. The inclusion of a book in the canon as well as its positioning and placement (ie questions of why and where) makes a difference in interpretation. This does not imply that the canonical order is authoritative. The question a canonical approach asks is not whether Moses wrote Genesis but rather what is the significance of the canonical text in ascribing the authorship of the Pentateuch to Moses. The obvious answer to that question seems to be that it gives the Pentateuch an authoritative status. Moreover, the theological value of the text is not tied to its historicity nor does the lack of historicity diminish its historical value. It also seeks to underscore the cumulative message of the entire collection and how their arrangement affect the way we construe the message of a book (eg Ecclesiastes). The canonical relationship is more important than chronology.

All texts are to be read in the light of other texts because the believing communities have accepted them as authoritative and normative for faith. Hence biblical texts may be read and interpreted as making theological claims and ethical demands. Rendtorff (1993a:29) has remarked that 'the strength of the canonical approach is its concern with larger units, such as biblical books, and even the canon as a whole.'

Finally, Childs has made a significant contribution to the contemporary church especially in the area of final form. Why is it so important? According to Childs (1979:75–76),

> The reason for insisting on the final form of Scripture lies in the peculiar relationship between the text and the people of God which is constitutive of the canon. The shape of the biblical text reflects a history of encounter between God and Israel. The canon serves to describe this peculiar relationship and to define the scope of this history by establishing a beginning and an end to the process . . . The significance of the final form of the biblical text is that it alone bears witness to the full history of revelation . . . The fixing of a canon of Scripture implies that the witness to Israel's experience with God lies in not recovering such historical process, but is testified to in the effect on the biblical text itself . . . It is only in the final form of the biblical text in which the normative history has reached an end that the full effect of this revelatory history can be perceived.

On the other hand, the canonical approach to hermeneutics has many critics.[24] One main criticism is his inconsistency and lack of clarity in the usage of the word canon. According to Barr (1983b:75–76), Childs' usage of the term canon has three meanings. It can refer to: (a) 'the list of books which together comprise the holy scripture'; (b) 'the final form of a book [ie canonical form] of a book, an individual book, as it stands in the bible'; and finally (c) 'a perspective, a way of looking at texts, a perception for which the term 'holistic' is often used'. Barr (ibid:79) goes on to say that Childs in using 'the one word "canon" for all three it is made to seem as if the valuations of (b) and (c) are rightly entailed by the factual and objective character of canon (a)'.

His usage of other terms like 'canonical process', 'canonical intentionality', 'canonical integrity', 'canon and scripture', etc are not clearly defined resulting in ambiguity.

Other criticisms include giving priority to the Hebrew canon rather than the Greek canon; making canon the primary context for interpretation since there is no historical precedent; subtle tendency to return to pre-critical hermeneutics, diminishing the importance of historical criticism and locating authority at the end of the canonical process rather than at the beginning.[25] By privileging the Masoretic text, he appears to down play any theological importance of other textual traditions. The plurality and diversity of voices that resonate in the texts and canon are smothered, synthesised and harmonised while dissonant texts are muffled (Barton 1984:85).

Whatever criticisms there may be, we need to remember that 'it is one programme for handling an authoritative scripture' (Auld)[26] It is therefore a viable option for doing hermeneutics.[27]

4.4 A Step in the Right Direction

Previously, scholars have paid careful attention to questions about the authentic form of the narratives and the original shape of the text. Scholars exude confidence in their abilities to restore the original texts by supposedly peeling off layers of alleged redaction.

But a paradigmatic shift has taken place with the synchronic approach surpassing (replacing?) the diachronic approach to interpretation. This has resulted in priority being given to the finished form of the biblical *oeuvre*. The final form approach is concerned with 'the architecture of individual narratives with artistic qualities, rhetorical characteristics, inner organisation, structural and stylistic features' (Kaiser 1995:70). The texts become the centre of concern with the character, structure, composition, content and theological status coming to the forefront.

Such an approach in its various formats are considered to be alternatives to historical criticism whose concern is with the history of events residing behind the texts or traditions.

Broadly speaking, two of the popular final form[28] approaches are *Canonical Criticism* which regards the Old Testament as Scripture (Brevard Childs' approach) and the other is *New Literary Criticism* which regards the Bible as literature (it includes a great variety of other literary methods).[29]

Both the Canonical criticism and the New criticism place emphasis on the form and content of biblical narratives. Both are critical of using biblical texts as a primary means to reconstruct the history and religion of Israel. The reason is that such endeavours in trying to detect the various sources and stages in redaction of early history are simply sophisticated guess works.[30] Furthermore, both approaches are strenuously opposed to the formulation of biblical/ theological ideas at the expense of the written texts. The common thread between both of these approaches is that meaning is not primarily located in the mind of the author but in the text itself.

4.5 The Viability of A Final Form Approach

The present day good news for biblical scholarship is that 'more scholars are viewing the final existing stage of the text as something that has an integrity and intention of its own' (Rendtorff 1993:51).[31] Similarly, Ryou

(1995:4–5) has also argued for the final text to be accorded 'legitimate entity' regardless of the extent of traditional and redactional layers.

In my judgement, a final form[32] approach to studying the biblical text is not only legitimate, viable but also essential for studying the biblical texts.

First, it is a needed correction to an age old principle in textual criticism that says the earlier the text, the more original it is. The reason is simple and understandable. 'An older text has a more objective and thus a higher value than later redaction or traditions, as if the older traditions are closer to the original revelation than the later ones' (Van Wolde 1994:171). However, Rendtorff (1994:3–14) has argued correctly that 'it is a mistake to say that "sources" are written by authors and therefore represent "original" text or even texts; but the contamination of these "original" texts has been made by editors, and therefore it is "secondary" (ibid:6). Moreover, the premise of the historical critical scholars that later layers added are to be peeled off has been recently challenged successfully by contemporary biblical scholars on literary and textual grounds. Hayman (1995:434–449) has argued that 'any search for the original text is a scholarly illusion since traditional material is shaped by community through the centuries.' This has been corroborated by Ulrich (1994:85) who has argued and demonstrated convincingly that 'composition-by-stages is the method by which scriptures were produced from the beginning' (we have manuscript evidence documenting two or more literary editions of some of the biblical books eg the Psalter). Since the text of each book was produced organically in multiple layers it is extremely difficult if not impossible to isolate 'the original text'(92).[33] Hence, there is no reason why an exegete should not begin with the text in its final (present) shape.

Secondly, the literary nature of the biblical text requires us to start with the givenness of the text as is done in all literary works. This also implies that a text may be understood without any reference to its pre-history or sources used.

Thirdly, the present form of the text provides a better foundation for exegetical activities since we have the text before us rather than a reconstructed text that is somewhat uncertain and difficult to reconstruct.[34] Rendtorff (1993b:48) correctly points out that 'it has been a long neglected task for exegesis to take the final form of the text seriously . . . instead of viewing that as a mere fortuitous product, or the outcome of the work of editors and augmenters, which has grown more or less uncontrolled.'

Fourthly, the final form approach provides a 'hermeneutical key to correct interpretation' because it 'performs a crucial hermeneutical function in establishing the peculiar profile of the passage' (Childs 1978:76–

77). Since biblical texts were shaped purposefully and purposely in order to function as a permanent theological witness,[35] it is only natural that theological meaning and authority be based on the final form of the text. On the other hand, if theological construction is based on reconstructed sources (which are speculative),[36] theologizing becomes equally hypothetical. As Moberly (1983:21) has so well stated,

> Whatever sources and different levels of meaning may underlie a text . . . they should be allowed no priority over the meaning of the text as it is now. On the contrary, the final text provides the norm for critical assessment of earlier levels of meaning.

Fifthly, since the final text was canonised, it became sacred, normative and authoritative in the Synagogue and the Church. 'It is in their final form (ie in the form they received from the redactors) that the books in the Old Testament exercise their influence on the community of believers' (Rendtorff 1991:128). Hence, by emphasising the final form of the text, the validity and veracity of theological truths need not be locked on to history.

Sixthly, one of the strengths of the final form approach (canonical/literary) is that nothing is incompatible even if it contains inconsistencies. Where difficulties arise, the first instinct is not to declare the text mutilated thereby reconstructing the text that fits the idea of the exegete but rather making an attempt to understand the text in its final form.[37]

Finally, it needs to be emphasized that a canonical reading operates with a specific theological agenda. The canon provides coherence of belief as well as protects the community from extraneous teaching. Texts are viewed as a whole and unified work. Without a canonical perimeter everything is permitted and there is no closure.

4.6 Summary

In spite of the current hermeneutical shift, some have continued to argue for the old historical paradigm. For them each time the death knell of historical criticism is sounded, it manages to rise in a newer or revised version like the mythical phoenix from the ashes. Perhaps it is more accurate to say that the old historical criticism is dead and a new historical criticism is reborn singing the same song but in a different tune. As Brueggemann (1997:105) perceptively observes, 'some will continue to champion its work, some out of profound conviction, and others out of wounds inflicted by authoritarian ecclesial community'.

Others have called for a synthesis of traditional methodologies and contemporary theories. One question that is constantly asked by exegetes is whether historical criticism and literary criticism can both tango to the same hermeneutical tune? According to Barton (1994:15) they both can and should. In his plea he says,

> It is in the interest of all students of Old Testament the historical and literary critics should somehow be brought to inhabit the same world, not to spend time staking out their own territory but to recognise the whole land lies before them, and that most of the texts they interpret need *both* historical *and* literary skill if they are to be adequately interpreted (italics his).

There are others who call for a distinct break between the historical and literary approaches because of their incompatibility.[38] They are incompatible because the diachronist and synchronist ask different questions (Greenstein 1988:353); they have different definitions concerning 'history' and they have different starting points as well as different points of reference. Those sets of literary and stylistic criteria used for identification of sources are incorporated 'into poetics of narrative that eschews the division of the materials into a variety of disparate sources' (Mullen 1997:3). Hence, they have different interpretive interests. Like oil and water, they do not mix. One who advocates a combination of the two approaches is essentially trying to step into two boats at the same time.[39]

There is a growing clarion call by some literary scholars to put to retirement the historical critical theory that has been floating around for too long. Scholars who still cling on to the old historical critical methods are said to be out of step with the new tune played by contemporary hermeneutics.

Be that as it may be, the literary crossing of the hermeneutical rubicon and the finished form approach to studying the biblical text have become the *Zeitgeist* of an academic fashion in vogue.[40] For some, it was like a breath of fresh air sweeping across the corridors of biblical studies; while others felt its impact was more like a hermeneutical *El Niño* disrupting the climate of historical criticism and dislodging their hegemony.

The sound of literary bells is growing louder than ever, amplified by the support of biblical scholars who have continued to challenge the old historical critical paradigm through publication. The radical literary critics, see the new(er) literary criticism as a bomb exploding in the playground of historical criticism. Because literary criticism is enjoying a wide currency, it appears today that when literary critics sneeze, biblical scholars seem to catch the literary flu very fast! This contagion effect is certainly felt even beyond the hermeneutical borders.

Many scholars have been bold to predict the demise of the historical critical method as inevitable and irreversible as more geological faultlines are admitted or discovered. Its infrastructure of cherished dogma is gradually dismantled by the bulldozer of literary and postmodern criticism.

Are the ominous clouds looming on the hermeneutical horizon signalling that historical criticism which began as a chapter in the academic world decades ago, may end up as a footnote in the history of interpretation by the end of this (next?) millennium?[41]

Notes

1   Biblical criticism is a broader term than historical criticism. For a brief but excellent understanding of the emergence of historical criticism, see Henning Graf Reventlow, *The Authority of the Bible and the Rise of Modern World* (trans. John Bowden; London: SCM, 1984); Klaus Scholder, *The Birth of Modern Critical Theology* (trans. John Bowden; London: SCM, 1990); Brueggemann (1997:9–15); Roy A. Harrisville and Walter Sundberg, *The Bible in Modern Culture: Theology and Historical-Critical Method from Spinoza to Kasemann* (Grand Rapids: Eerdmans, 1995) and Mary Sanford, 'An orthodox View of Biblical criticism', *Epiphany Journal* 11/2 (1991): 36–41; Stephen Prickett, *Origins of Narrative: The Romantic Appropriation of the Bible* (Cambridge: Cambridge University Press, 1996); Gerald Bray, *Biblical Interpretation: Past and Present* (Downers Grove. Illinois: Intervarsity press, 1996) especially 225–460; Peter Harrison, *The Bible, Protestantism and the Rise of Natural Science* (Cambridge: Cambridge University Press, 1997).

2   On the impact and Influence of the Enlightenment, see Stanley J. Grenz and Roger E. Olson, *20th Century Theology: God and the World in a Transitional Age* (Downers Grove, Illinois: Intervarsity Press, 1992:15–23 and John Kent, 'The Enlightenment' in Peter Byrne and Leslie Houlden (eds), *Companion Encyclopedia of Theology* (London: Routledge, 1995): 251–271.

3   For a helpful discussion on the concept of Enlightenment, consult Issac Kramnick (ed), *The Portable Enlightenment Reader* (London: Penguin Books, 1995).

4   Epistemologically, there arose 'a new model of knowledge grounded on objectivity, and capable of providing a new epistemological security to replace that which was lost in the dissolution of the Medieval world' (Bordo 1987:76). This is a positive contribution because in the new worldview endeavours to provide stability and certainty through empirical demonstration and rationalism.

5   See Holladay (1994):128–131.

6   See the critiques of Gerhard Maier, *The End of Historical Critical Method* (trans. Edwin W. Leverenz and Rudolf F. Norden; St. Louis: Publishing House, 1974; Eta Linneman, *Historical Criticism: Methodology or Ideology* (trans. Robert W. Yarbrough; Grand Rapids: Baker Book House, 1990); J. D. Levenson, *The Hebrew Bible, the Old Testament, and Historical Criticism* (Westminster: John Knox, 1993) and Carl E. Braaten and Robert W. Jenson (eds), *Reclaiming the Bible for the Church* (Grand Rapids: Eerdmans, 1995).

7   Cf James Dunn, 'A Word in Time', in *Epworth Review* 19/2 (1992):27–42.

8   Even Bloom (1991:44) in his book entitled *The Book of J* radically proposes that J is a sophisticated lady from aristocratic line. However, he concedes that,

> Recovering J will not throw light on Torah or on the Hebrew Bible or on the Bible of Christianity. I do not think that appreciating J will help us love God or arrive at the spiritual or historical truth of whatever Bible.

See Harold Bloom *The Book of J*, trans. David Rosenberg (London: 1991).

9   See Lim (1997):100–105.

10   Whenever there are parallel passages, it is difficult to know who borrows from whom. Therefore, it is risky to specify the process by which one copies from the other.

At best we can say that there are some internal relations between the texts. In any case, from the narrative viewpoint, it is not important to know who borrows from whom. Neither does it ask which text comes first.

11   For an elaboration of this point, see Levenson (1993).

12   For a detailed critique of historical criticism see Edgar W. Conrad, 'Reflections on Biblical Reflections', in *Australian Religion Studies Review* 8/1 (1995) 2–3 and also his book on *Reading Isaiah* (OBT 27; Minneapolis: Fortress Press, 1991) 3–27. Cf also Conrad's apt metaphor of the historical critical scholars' (over?)emphasis on authorial intention and historical background as 'frozen waterfall', pg 24.

13   William Johnston quoted by Campbell in 'Past History and Present Text: The Clash of Classical & Post Critical Approach to Biblical Text,' *ABS* Vol 39 (1991) 1–18 especially p 1.

14   What is the relationship between poststructuralism and historical criticism? According to Moore (1994:117),

> . . . Poststructuralism is temperamentally unsuited to be yet another handmaid (a French handmaid?) to historical criticism. Neither is poststructuralism poised to become historical criticism's slayer (historical criticism is much too massive for that, occupying entire city blocks at the national conferences; it crushes its enemies by sitting on them). Rather, in the context of biblical studies, poststructuralism would be historical criticism's id, the seat of its strongest anti authoritarian instincts-historical criticism unfettered at last from the ecclesiastical superego that has compelled it to genuflect before the icons it had come to destroy.

15   Within the literary critics there are also great differences eg. Ryken & Frye. See the excellent discussion by Robert A Weathers, 'Leland Ryken's Approach to Biblical Interpretation, An Evangelical Model,' *Journal of the Evangelical Theological Society* 37/1 (March 1994) 115–124.

16   I am in agreement with Hall (1995:371, footnote 2) who says that ever since the classic publication of Brevard Childs, *Introduction to Old Testament as Scripture* (Phildelphia: Fortress, 1979), Childs has not added any new substantial material to his 'canonical approach'.

Note also that the most outstanding triumvirate of the Yale School (considered by many to be a postliberal movement) are Childs, Lindbeck and Frei with strong emphasis on the biblical text and Jesus Christ by whom all other reality is be constructed. It gives prominence also to the primacy of the narrative as an interpretive category; to the world created by biblical narratives instead of the world of human experience and language takes precedence over experience.

17   For a critique of Frei's position, see Leo G. Perdue, *The Collapse of History: Reconstructing Old Testament Theology* (OBT; Minneapolis: Fortress Press, 1994):259–262.

18   The view of Ulrich (1992b:267–272) on the canon is very plausible. His views are summarised here.

       The word canon is postbiblical. It is a technical term with an established usage in theological discourse. The issue of canon is both a historical and theological issue. The word canon represents a reflexive judgement; it denotes a closed list, and it concerns the biblical books. It is generally agreed that there is no canon as such in Judaism before the end of the first century C.E. or in Christianity before the fourth century. This implies that prior to the late first century C.E., either in Judaism or in Christianity, there is no evidence to suggest that there was neither a fixed list of books, or a fixed test either of individual books or a unified collection of books.

       At best we can say that there was a canon-in-the-making but we do not have a canon. Instead what we have is a well documented by practice, the concept of authoritative sacred books which are to be preserved very faithfully. And we have a "canonical process" that is, the activity by which the books later become accepted as the canon were produced and treated as sacred and authoritative.

       Although within rabbinic Judaism, the Masoretic stream of textual tradition is seen to be the only legitimate textual form of the canonical books, there may be evidence to show that diaspora Judaism or even widespread Palestinian Judaism generally accepted, prior to the middle third of the second century, the proto-Masoretic stream. Prior to the end of the first century Torah and the Prophets were accepted as authoritative while writings were accepted authoritative in part. In other words, there was a category of scared, authoritative books to which further entries could be added, and that category contained a number of books which were always included and always required to be included (the five Books of Moses, Isaiah, Psalms etc.) even though others could also be included (Ezekiel, Song, Ester, Jubilees etc).

19   Childs is of the opinion that early in Israel's historical existence (Deut 31:24f; 2 Kings 22; the law of Ezra; Isa 8:16; Jeremiah 36), there was already an awareness of certain sacred writings which he calls 'canon consciousness'. By the second century BCE, the Pentateuch and the prophets reached canonical status while the writings became canonical by the beginning of the CE.

20   Childs is right to insist that even though some early traditions were considered sacred, once the canonical process was completed only the final form of the texts were considered authoritative for the communities of faith.

21   The difference between a historical critic and a canonical critic has been explained this way. A historical critic enters a room full of paintings and begins to

arrange them in chronological order and asks questions about historical circumstances that led to their paintings. On the other hand, a canonical critic accepts the paintings for what they are and look at them in their own rights and tries to make sense for what they are. See Carl Holladay, 'Contemporary Methods of Reading the Bible', in Leander E. Keck, Thomas Long, et al. (eds), *The New Interpreter's Bible* (vol 1; Nashville: Abingdon, 1994):125–149.

22   For a recent study of the early Church use of Old Testament, see Craig A. Evans and James Sanders, *Early Christian Interpretation of Scriptures of Israel: Investigations and Proposals* (JSNTSup, 148; England: Sheffield, 1997).

23   Sanders (1995:62) prefers the term canonical criticism. For him what is significant about canon is not the final form of the text but the process by which the community arrived at the form. The canonical process began way back at the first repetition/recital in oral tradition and continues beyond closure till today. The function of Scripture as canon is to provide the paradigm whereby the process is discerned and continues in believing communities till today. Scripture does not offer eternal truths or theological doctrines but a set of stories of how believing communities find life in those stories.

     Childs on the other hand, sees canon as referring to literary texts that become normative of those events to which it bore witness. The closure of the canon and the final form of the text is important for the discernment of the hermeneutics of the text. Therefore a canonical text refers to the historically final and normative form of the text. Sanders is more concerned with the canonical process while Childs is more concerned with the canonical product (Callaway 1993:125–126).

     Put simply, Childs highlights 'textual stability' while Sanders spotlights on 'contextual adaptability' (Wall 1995: footnote 6).

24   One of the strongest critics to the canonical approach is James Barr. It seems that the force of Barr's arguments appears to be weakened (though not demolished) in the light of Topping's (1992:239–260) as well as Provan's (1997:1–38) rebuttals and others.

     For a balanced critique, see Dale A Brueggeman, "Brevard Child's Canon Criticism: An Example of Post Critical Naivete" in *Journal of Evangelical Theological Society* 32/3 (Sept 1989) 311–326; Leo G. Perdue, *The Collapse of History: Reconstructing Old Testament Theology* (OBT; Minneapolis: Fortress Press, 1994):182–196 and J. Dickson Brown, "Barton Books and Childs: A comparison of the New Criticism and Canonical Criticism" in *Journal of Evangelical Theological Society* 36/4 (Dec 1993) 481–485. He argues that the canonical approach bears superficial resemblance to the New criticism which emphasizes on the text itself, indifference to authorial intention, integration of individual texts into a literary canon.

     Charles J Scalise, "Canonical Hermeneutics: Childs & Barth" in *SJT* vol 47 (1994) 61–88 argues that Barthian hermeneutics provides appropriate theological context for understanding Child's canonical approach.

     See also Rolf Rendtorff, *Canon & Theology,* (trans. Margaret Kohl; Minneapolis: Fortress Press, 1993) especially 46–56 and Samuel Cheon, 'B.S. Childs' Debate with Scholars about His Canonical Approach', *Asia Journal of Theology* 11:2 (1997):343–357.

For a New Testament Perspective, see Robert W. Wall, 'Reading the New Testament in Canonical Context', in Joel Green (ed), *Hearing the New Testament* (Grand Rapids, Michigan: William B. Eerdmans, 1995):370–393.

According to Sanders (1995:60), Barr's strong rhetoric opposition to canonical approaches 'betrays nonetheless a kind of insensitivity to the inroads of indeterminacy in deconstructive post-modernism and the considerable doubts now cast on theoretical reconstructions of the history of the formation of biblical literature.'

It is a fair statement to say that in spite of Barr's attempt to silence the canon adherents with his cannon of obstreperous verbal volleys, the canonical approach has gained more adherents.

25   In fairness to Childs, he does not deny that the earlier stages in a book's development could have been authoritative and normative when they were first shaped. However, what ultimately counts is the final stage when the texts were canonized. Moreover, he does accept the fact that tensions do resonate within a text or the entire canon.

26   A paper entitled 'Word of God and Word of Man', read by Professor Graeme Auld at the New College opening function on 24th October 1984.

27   For a broader understanding of the canon and its implications, see Fornberg (1986:45–53), Brett (1991), Lightston (1979:135–142), Morgan (1990:11–29), Childs (1992-55–79; 719–727), Bruns (1984:462–480), Letis (1991:261–277) Harris (1991:110–121) and Miller (1994). See also James A. Sanders, 'Scripture as Canon for Post-Modern Times' *Biblical Theological Bulletin* 25/2 (1995):56–64.

For a recent and detailed assessment of Child's canonical approach where central issues such as historical, hermeneutical and theological are identified (in terms of strengths and weaknesses) as well as some suggestions given on how to put the canonical approach on a firmer methodological footing, see Paul R. Noble, *The Canonical Approach: A Critical Reconstruction of the Hermeneutics of Brevard Childs* (Leiden: E. J. Brill, 1995).

28   It is understandable why historical critical scholars who are trying to reconstruct the Urtext in its pristine form feel uncomfortable with the term final form of the text.

I am aware of the controversies surrounding the term canonical texts, final text, etc. By using the term 'final form' we have also opened a few cans of textual worms for the textual critics. Questions such as the history of textual transmission, final redaction, textual stabilisation, glosses, stabilisation of texts, textual witnesses, etc. will be raised.

It is beyond the scope of this research to deal with all the intricacies of this complex topic as well as to discuss all the ramifications except to say that the general concept of the final form of the text is clear. It can and could be used as a starting point because 'nothing can be done unless we start with it as a heuristic principle' (Frye, quoted by Moberly,1983:19).

The phrase final form is a universally accepted and important term across all interdisciplinary studies. Essentially, this term means that all texts are to be accorded with integrity and understood on their own terms. That is to say that the focal point of interpretive acts should be on the *received text* rather than *reconstructed text*. Other expressions such as 'present text', 'given text', etc. have also been used.

Owing to its widespread usage, the term final form should be used in biblical studies (with a caveat) if biblical scholars are to communicate with literary scholars.

29   A third possible approach is to combine both. Consult Lim (1997:41) footnote 86 for books on literary approaches.

30   Some would even insist that even if the original context of the text could be reconstructed, it does not add any new value to the meaning of the text because texts have meanings of their own apart from their historical contexts.

31   Other than Childs and Rendtorff we can also include other luminaries like Sternberg, Steiner, Fishbane, Blum, Levenson, etc.

32   The idea of a final text is unsettling in light of the Dead Sea Scrolls discovery of the different Text types. A distinction must be made between a final text and a final form of the text. The former seems to suggest uniformity and the existence of only one Text type. Whereas the latter admits the existence of different Text types with each one of them reaching a point of stabilization at different periods. While no one can be certain when it happened, everyone is sure it did happen.

It was Franz Rosenzweig who first stated that *R* stands not only for Redactor but *Rabbenu* (our master). Since we have received the text from the hands of these last writers, we must listen to their voices and messages first.

33   Some of the difficult questions posed by Ulrich concerning 'the original text' are worth pondering. How do we decide which of the many layers that could claim to be the 'original reading' to select? Often the richer religious meanings in a text are those which entered the text at a relatively late or developed stage; do we choose the earlier, less rich reading or the later, more profound reading? In contrast, if a profound religious insight in an early stage of the text is toned down later by a standard formula or even a vapid platitude, which do we select? And must we not be consistent in choosing the early or the later edition or reading (Ulrich 1994:92–93)?

34   It is needs to be emphasised that most, if not all practitioners of final form (received text) exegesis, acknowledges the importance of the text's prehistory but is more concerned with the finished composition. Rather than focusing on the history behind the text or history prior to the text, it concentrates on the history of the text as it acquired canonical status. The reason is that the final form represents a final stage in the community's theological reflection.

35   In the final analysis, plurivocity gives way to univocity since biblical texts have one univocal Subject—God.

36   Rendtorff (1994:3–14) in speaking of the Pentateuch has reminded us again that Pentateuchal sources are merely scholarly reconstruction and not realities. All sources like Yahwist, Elohist, Priestly, etc. do not exist outside the intellectual minds of the scholars and the thousands of books scholars have written on these

sources. This means that Bible scholars usually interpret texts they themselves or other scholars before them have reconstructed, not to say, fabricated (ibid: 5).

37   Cf. also James Dunn (1987:62) who argues for the final form approach. In his judgement, the final form approach gives the clearest norm against which to judge speculative reconstructions of earlier stages; it is most accessible to normal believers and is the form in which the text arose out of the mass of competing traditions to original prominence and has persisted throughout the centuries. See *The Living Word* (London:SCM, 1987) especially pages 162, 172–173 and 150.

38   See Paul Noble, 'Scripture and Diachronic Approaches to Biblical Interpretation', *Literature and Theology* 7/2 (1993):130–148.

39   I recall an anecdote about the American civil war when the North and the South were fighting. One soldier was in a dilemma because he wanted to please both sides. He came out with a brilliant idea. He decided to wear a blue suite and a grey trousers to show his neutrality. But fate would not have it. He was shot from both sides! Is there a parable for scholars in this story, I wonder?

40   For introduction, see Mark Minor, *Literary Critical Approaches to the Bible* (West Cornwall, CT: Locust Hill Press, 1992); Mark Allan Powell, et al., *The Bible and Modern Literary Criticism* (New York: Greenwood Press, 1992); Alex Preminger and Edward Greenstein (eds), *The Hebrew Bible in Literary Criticism* (New York: Ungar, 1986) and Duane F. Watson and Alan J. Hauser, *Rhetorical Criticism of the Bible: A Comprehensive Bibliography with Notes on History and Method* (Leiden: E.J. Brill, 1994).

41   It remains to be seen whether a single methodology is going to emerge as the predominant paradigm.

Chapter Five

A Theory of Textuality

When Philip ran up he heard him reading from the prophet Isaiah and asked, 'Do you understand what you are reading?' He said, 'How can I without someone to guide me?' (Acts 8:30)

5.1 Text-Oriented Approach

In my view, the text oriented approach scores very high as a candidate for biblical interpreters amidst competing strategies. This textual mode has more potential rather than problems.[1] What is a text oriented approach? According to Sternberg (1985:15), a text centred approach

. . . sets out to understand not the realities behind the text but the text itself as a pattern of meaning and effect. What does this piece of language-metaphor, epigram, dialogue, tale, cycle book-signify in context? What are the rules governing the transaction between the story teller or poet and reader?. . . What image of a world does the narrative project? Why does it unfold the action in this particular order and from this particular viewpoint? What is the part played by the omissions, redundancies, ambiguities, alternations between scene and summary or elevated and colloquial language? How does the work hang together? And, in general, in what relationship does part stand to whole and form to function?

A textual approach is essentially an attempt to interpret and understand the textual constituents without external reference. It is both an art and a science, a theory and practice. Understanding of its textual meaning as expressed in a written language is achieved using linguistic and literary tools during a dialogical encounter between the interpreter and the text leading to a fusion of horizons.

Thiselton (1980:445) is right when he asserts

The hermeneutical goal is that of a steady progress towards a fusion of horizons. But this is to be achieved in such a way that the particularity of each horizon is fully taken into account and respected. This means both respecting the rights of the text and allowing it to speak.

Rowland (1995:430-431;435) adds his voice by saying

> . . . fruitful exegesis involves acknowledgement of the importance of the two poles (text and reader). . . [where] there is an interaction between reader(s) and their context and the text and its context . . . The two dimensions of interpretation, the text and its context, and the readers and their context are both necessary. To do justice to the texts and their effects necessitates that both poles should be taken seriously.

Interpretation is a dynamic process between the reader and the text in which the text does something to the reader.

While the focus of author-approach is on the past, and the reader-oriented is on the present, the text-centred methodology deals adequately with the past and present. A textual approach is best suited to mediate between the text and its readers.

According to McKnight (1993:205), 'when the Bible is approached as both an ancient document with original meaning and a living message with contemporary significance, the bridge to a comprehensive and satisfying biblical hermeneutics may have been found.' In my opinion, the textual approach encapsulates that.

The text is read as a unified whole so as to pay close attention to the strategies employed by the narrator and how the overall structure and its constituent parts contribute to the meaning of the text. In other words, 'what is the big picture presented in the text' (Rogerson's phrase).

The text oriented approach seeks to mediate between throwing the authorial water in the hermeneutical bath tub along with the textual baby. Having said that, the textual approach does not deny the important role an author plays. I see the authorial intention as a factor to be considered but not essential to the evaluation of his work.

According to Halivni (1991:n 5),

> authorial intention remains an important component, perhaps the single most important component of any interpersonal communication. It may not exhaust all of the meaning. But neither is meaning meaningful without it. It remains central.

Although the author's statement of meaning may have heuristic value, it cannot be the determining factor in discerning the meaning of his text. In other words, 'authorial intention is at best a requirement of reading and therefore a partial goal of interpretation, rather than a key that unlocks valid meaning' (Scholes 1985:49–50).

While external data may be drawn from evidence to show his usage of certain words, it must not be the decisive factor in interpreting the text. The author's purpose functions as a regulative principle for correct interpretation, and is indisputable for fixing the proper context of interpretation.

In a sense, the author is not present, the text is an independent entity and the author no longer controls it. However, we have an ethical responsibility not to make the text mean what we wish. As Young & Ford (1987:87) remark, 'you cannot make a text mean anything you like and the author's intention has some primacy in determining meaning'.

At the same time the text oriented approach seeks to maintain the integrity of language and determinacy of meaning. 'If meaning is not in the text, then reading is like dropping buckets into an empty well.' says Vanhoozer.

In this way we avoid the two extreme views of authorial intention being irrelevant and that authorial intention is decisive.

Finally, the premise of working with the givenness of the text, its clarion call for respecting the textual unity and integrity; its textual and contextual constraints as the parameters for exegesis; its emphasis on confronting the text and being challenged by it; the due right given to the ancient context without ignoring the modern context; validation of interpretation being circumscribed by the text; the dialectical relationship between the reader and the text; and seeing the text as sense—these are good reasons enough to use the text oriented approach.

5.1.1 Implications

First, attention is given to the biblical texts as objects of beauty and meaning, rather than to the author or events behind them. It is the text, not the one who wrote it, that is the focus of interpretation. Moroever, the authorship of ancient texts is problematic. The text is not a means of obtaining an understanding of the identity, thought, and life of the author, or anything else outside the text itself. Meaning and reference are both internal to the text. This assertion challenges and undermines the efforts of historical criticism.

Second, the biblical text and not the author is the source and judge of the propriety of an interpretation. Not much importance is placed on the intention of the author (Belsey 1980:15–20).

Third, meaning is a function of the position a text holds within a literary context. Texts have cultural fields of reference that impact their meaning. Nevertheless, the specificity of a text's meaning, and not the diffused cultural values, is the focus of interpretation. That is to say the meaning of a text should come from within its own narrative reality, not its location in some external field of discourse.

Finally, I concur with Wright (1982:64) in his affirmations of the text.

> First we can affirm both that the text does have a particular viewpoint from which everything is seen, and at the same time that the reader's reading is not mere 'neutral observation'. Second, we can affirm both that the text has a certain life of its own, and that the author has intentions of which we can in principle gain at least some knowledge. Third, we can affirm both that the actions or objects described may well be, in principle, actions and objects in the public world and that the author was looking at them from a particular, and perhaps, distorting point of view. At each level we need to say both-and, not just either or.

5.2 A Need for Theory

A textual theory (theoretical framework)[2] is needed where texts can be defined and distinguished from non text. In formulating a textual theory,[3] I will seek to build a broad theoretical base that interprets, evaluates as well as integrates other relevant textual theories.[4] A conceptual structure is improvised first in order to develop a set of categories or constructs that will enable me to describe textual phenomena and the forces behind them.[5] Through linkage, a set of propositions is obtained.

The causal and symbiotic relationship between exegesis and theory is accentuated by Todorov (1981:viii) who says

> Exegesis always presupposes a theory (however unconscious), for it needs descriptive concepts, or more simply a vocabulary, in order to refer to the work studies; now, definitions of concepts are precisely what constitutes theory. But theory also presupposes the existence of exegesis, for it is by means of exegesis that theory contact with the substance that serves as its point of departure: literary discourse itself.

A theory has been likened to a map where the topographical contours and geographical terrains may be described *truly* but not *completely*. Though it shows how the various elements on the map are related to one another, none of them are real countries but are useful in describing particularities. A structure of a theory also helps to determine the function a theory can or cannot perform. The establishment of a delimitation will ensure that the structure will not break down under its own weight of explanation.

A theory is a framework that enables an interpreter to see the text from a certain perspective. However, it does not prescribe once and for all authoritative rules. The usefulness of a theory is measured by its simplicity and comprehensiveness.[6] It has been argued that without an ample theory, there can be no accurate interpretation of the biblical texts (Ferguson 1986:83).[7] In sum, a theory of textual interpretation is basically a theory on reading the text sensitively and strategically.

5.3 Axioms of a Text Centred Approach

I   **A text is a record of sentences written purportedly to be meaningful, unified and coherent with a definable communicative function.[8]**

How is a text defined?[9] A text is a 'medium of discourse' (Fowler 1986:85) fixed by writing with a communicative function.[10] It has linguistic semantic entities in which explicit statements and their presuppositions interact' (Knierim 1992:1). The linguistic identity of the text is its communicative perspective and its structure. The style expressed is not mere ornamentation but expression of individuality.

Texts are structured wholes or ordered composition which asks the readers for response. A text may be metaphorically extended to include messages generated by sign-systems as traffic signals, religious or civic rituals, styles of dress, non-verbal body-language,or electronically coded indicators (Thiselton 1992:55). The property of the text is its texture and this is what distinguishes a text from non text. It is a discourse fixed by writing with an ontological and epistemological starting point.

A written text may simply be said to be a collection of letters and symbols (Hieroglyphics, alphabet, greek symbols, characters). They can be written on papyrus, skins, stones, etc. Meaning on the other hand is a product of reasoning and thought.

Every text has its own properties. According to Beaugrande and Dressler (1981:48–286), several of the elements include cohesion (mutual connection of words within a sequence on the surface level), coherence (components of the textual world are mutually accessible and relevant on the deep level or subtext), intentionality (author centred), acceptability (reader's receptivity to the textual meaning), informativity (the extent to which the occurrences of the presented text are expected), situationality (factors that render a text relevant to a current situation), and intertextuality (the ways in which the production and reception of a given text depends upon the participant's knowledge of the other texts).

Furthermore, according to Lotman (1977:50–56), a text is characterised by:

a) Expression—a text expresses through signs of natural language
b) Demarcation—is inherent in a text and each text is defined by the reader according to a set of features. A text possesses an indivisible text meaning.
c) Structure —inherent in a text which is an internal organisation which transforms on the syntagmatic level into a structural whole.

In sum, a text is a set of written sentences that is grammatically, semantically and sequentially structured with a communicative function.[11] A text not only carries information but also should be seen as a strategy of communication designed by the writer to lead the reader to a path of understanding through the placement of clues or hints in strategic places in the text. The reader who follows those clues can gain correct understanding of the message. Wilson (1993:101) remarks that 'every text is not only an argument by an author about a subject matter, it is also for the sake of some end or purpose or function.' Furthermore, 'every text is not only a perspective on a reality but says something about the reality from this perspective. What it says about the reality will have some kind of order or structure or form or correlatedness or argument or method' (71).[12]

Recognising the genre of the text helps in comprehension too. On the other hand, at times the writer may want to be ambiguous but by and large a text is written with an aim of communicating messages for readers to understand.

II A linguistic knowledge of grammatical structure and vocabulary usage assist in interpretation[13] while other text forming devices like words and phrases enable sentences[14] to cohere[15] in a text.

A text is written by someone in a particular language. A text does not suddenly appear in history or out of nowhere. An author uses language to formulate a text which is a product of a particular culture or age. 'The text is historical in its origin, having its birth within a complex of social, literary, linguistic, and ideological systems, certain limits are automatically placed upon the reader of the text' (Tate 1991:7).

Through his knowledge of linguistic conventions, the writer expresses his meaning. Communication and comprehension are possible because societies agree to use words in accordance with certain conventions. Thus when a text is read in an alien environment, the text becomes meaningless. Words do not have meanings on their own but rather they are developed by people.[16]

Language is by nature a structured system which functions on the basis of human conventions. Because any language system is dependent on conventions of language, it is subject to change.[17]

III The context of a biblical text fulfils a vital function in textual interpretation because meaning is context bound.

Baldick (1990:45) defines contexts as:

> Those parts of a text preceding and following any particular passage, giving it a meaning fuller or more identifiable than if it were read in isolation. The context of any statement may be understood to comprise immediately neighbouring signs (including punctuation such as quotation marks), or any part of—or the whole of -the remaining text, or the biographical, social, cultural, and historical circumstances in which it is made (including the intended audience or reader).[18]

A knowledge of how the context delineates and defines the text will ensure accurate exegesis. The aphorism still rings true that a text without a context is simply a pretext! In the comprehension of a passage and construction of meaning, the elements of textuality, intertextuality and intratextuality play very significant roles because biblical texts refer to each other diachronically, chronologically, semiotically and semantically. The limit to the application of a contextual approach is the Canon.

Linguistically, there are three types of context (Fowler 1986:86–101).

- Context of Utterance—the situation within which the discourse is conducted, eg. place, surroundings.
- Context of Culture—the whole network of social and economic conventions and institutions constituting the culture at large.
- Context of Reference—the topic or subject matter of the text.

A text potentially has 'an undifferentiated whole of possibilities and a reader uses a number of the possibilities as a basis of his giving of meaning' (Van Wolde 1994:174). The availability of possible meanings is great because of the polysemic structure of the elements of the text. Any correct textual disambiguation depends on understanding the context. A word may assume many meanings but once they are situated within a particular context their possibilities are limited. As Eco (1990:41) points out 'even though the interpreters cannot decide which interpretation is the privileged one, they can agree on the fact that certain interpretations are not contextually legitimated.'Therefore it is the context that is determinative of the text's meaning because 'context conditions and constrains usage' (Loughlin 1995:334). In other words, since 'every text has a context which the interpreter must respect and not ride roughshod over its perspective but placing himself with it' (Noble 1991:269).

The context is established by the interaction of syntagmatic and paradigmatic relationship within the system. The syntagma deal with the relationship between words in the same paragraph and sentences while the paradigms deal with relation of words to others in the code which might have been used as substitutes. While symbols may be ambiguous within the paradigm but never within the syntagm. Words are seen to have no meaning apart from their linguistic context but to be understood 'only as a part of a whole'.

In biblical interpretation, we have to understand the texts in their historical context before we can use them to inform our contemporary context. By ignoring the historical context, the integrity of the biblical text is affected; while ignoring contemporary context, the human's contribution to understanding is overlooked. The key to this dilemma is learning to balance both contexts.

Dunn (1995:344-345) phrases it this way:

> The words of the text are like the innumerable small roots and tendrils which attached it to that soil. To attempt to transplant that plant by ripping it clear from its native soil and shaking it free from that soil may work, but it is likely to kill the plant . . . So with a historical text. The words of a historical text root it in the historical context out of which it first grew, and unless it carries with it something at least of that historical context, it is unlikely to survive any transplant into a different (contemporary) context.

IV The starting point for interpretation is the present text rather than the reconstruction of the Urtext.

The focus of interpretation should be on the text as it now exists rather than attempting to discuss the process through which the text comes into existence because sources are irrecoverable though traceable.[19]

Meaning of a text is inseparable from the form in which it is expressed. Therefore, meaning in a text is not found behind the text in the events which it ostensibly refers to, nor in the cultural or religious situations which produced them.

The text is viewed as a self contained entity and as an end in itself. The focus of attention shifts from the past to the present and historical information is subordinated to literary interests.

V The textual artifact must be taken seriously[20] and viewed holistically[21] while recognising the interdependence between the text and the interpreter.

In any interpretive endeavour, we should not seek to dissect the text but rather we should try to discern the thread that holds the text together. The text is to be understood on its own terms because there is a parameter set by the text! Hence, the unity of the text is emphasized. As Jeanrond (1988:3) argues,

> to refuse to consider the primacy of textual understanding would mean to expose oneself right from the beginning to the possibility of denying the importance of that which constitutes the sustaining success of theological thought, namely the text.

McEvenue (1994:495) also remarks that 'interpretation is a spiral activity, moving from element to whole and from whole to element, but never moving to a historical reality outside the literary work itself.' The horizon of the text forms the counterpoint of the horizon of the reader and the tension between the two opens the possibility of a new understanding which requires openness and courage. The dictum of Bengel still stands: Apply yourself to the Text and apply its substance to Yourself (*Te totum applica ad textum rem totam applica ad te*).

Meaning is posited in the text which can be elicited or objectively discovered through challenging the texts and letting the texts challenge us. Textual intention is not sought outside or behind but in the text.[22] The literal sense *(sensus literalis)* is usually intended unless otherwise indicated. Thus the reader need not perform 'any intricate or critical operations upon the text or wrest from it meaning' (Wood 1981:40). The reader moves from understanding of the text to understanding through the text ie, from a 'knowledge of the text to knowledge which the text fosters' (Wood ibid:42).[23]

VI Texts have determinate meaning that resides in them which can be grasped when the text and the interpreter share something in common called preunderstanding (presuppositions).

The role of preunderstanding was recognised a long time ago but has been given prominence recently.

As Morgan and Barton (1989:40) maintain:

> Historical and linguistic study help interpreters to bridge the distance in time and culture that separate them from the Bible. But it is no substitute for some prior understanding of the biblical subject-matter. Every reader needs some foothold in the text being studied, some preliminary grasp of what it is about before understanding can take place.

Tate (1991:163) also affirms that

> every reader approaches a text under the guidance of a perspective. Any text is read, perceived and interpreted with a pre-existent structure of reality. All understanding and interpretation proceed from a prior understanding of a system of making sense of reality.

What is preunderstanding? It is 'a body of assumptions and attitudes which a person brings to the perception and interpretation of reality or any aspect of it' (Ferguson 1986:6). The four components of preunderstanding include information, attitude, ideology and methodology (ibid:13–14).[24]

Broadly speaking, a preunderstanding can be described as a personal construct, worldview paradigm, belief system, presupposition or simply one's prior understanding of the subject. It also refers to questions and concerns interpreters bring to the text that will determine the shape of the interpretation. None can approach a text without some kind of theological or ideological predisposition. Our questions to the text are formed within our horizon of expectation and prejudices. Openness to the text is obtained by bringing our prejudices into play critically and not by ignoring them (Gadamer 1975:151–152). Hence the words of Young and Ford (1987:135) are very important:

> If interpretation is to have integrity, it must attend to these complexities and be critically aware of presuppositions, inherent in the interpreter as well as in the text. The interpreter with dogmatic interests invested in the outcome, is likely to distort the message to suit personal and community interest.

Preunderstanding has several significant implications for hermeneutics:

First, all reading is theory laden because we do not read texts as they are but we read texts as we are. That is to say we read texts only as we perceive them to be. There is no "innocent" reading because all reading is ideologically motivated. Each reader comes to the text with a particular frame of reference coloured by past experiences through which he interprets the text. In other words, 'we are not neutral observers and never can be, and ought not to pretend that we are' (Ziesler 1994:273).[25]

Secondly, all understanding presupposes preunderstanding. As Scholes (1985:48) remarks,

> Reading is only possible to the extent the reader shares a semantic and syntactic field (a set of codes and to paradigms that enable and constrain meaning) with the writer. The further estranged the reader is from the writer (time, space, language), the more interpretation must be called upon to provide a conscious construction of unavailable or faded codes and paradigms.

Our answers are determined by the questions we ask. Without prior understanding on the part of the interpreter, the meaning of the text cannot be understood. No one comes to the text as a *tabula rasa* since we live in a concrete historical situation. Palmer's point (1969:251) is relevant:

> When interpreting a text from a past age, the interpreter does not empty his mind or leave the present absolutely : he takes it with him and uses it to understand in the dialectical encounter of his horizons with that of the literary work.

Long (1987:168) is on target when he claims,

> The interpreter neither pretends to have objectivity nor desires to have neutrality toward the text. The confessional willingness to give consent to the text is not a barrier to interpretation. It is the only true way into the text.

Thirdly, part of preunderstanding/understanding rests on the capacity to understand the genre. 'When a reader cannot accept the convention of a particular genre, a work simply becomes unintelligible' says Mazzeo (1978:23). Furthermore, Morgan & Barton (1989:4) add that 'it is important to recognise what kind of text one is reading and what literary devices are being employed. How we clarify it (the literary 'genre') will decide how we read it.'

Fourthly, subjectivity cannot be avoided. As Gadamer (1975:153) correctly states that 'the aim of the interpreter is not to eliminate subjectivity, which is impossible, but to become critically aware of it, to train it and to check it out as thoroughly as possible and objectivity and subjectivity be kept in balance. . .' Mazzeo (1971:22) argues that a 'text must be understood 'subjectively' or existentially if it is to be understood authentically.'

Fifthly, preunderstanding can function positively or negatively. The question is: will the reader confronted by the text's invitation and challenge respond or rebel, respect or suspect, submit or resist? Our preunderstanding is enabling and limiting. It can open a work in a particular way and close off potential modes of access. 'Because our preunderstanding can function positively (understanding) or negatively (distorting the image of the text) . . . distanciation is important because it protects the reader from the text and the text from the reader' (Schneiders 1991:169).

In the process of interpretation, our presuppositions which govern our interpretation may be altered, changed or strengthened by new answers generating new understanding. Since preunderstanding is related to the "hermeneutical circle" which is unavoidable, however authentic our reading of a text may be, only a particular aspect of it is given to the reader to understand at a particular point of time and space. Hence, 'what is decisive is not to get out of the circle but to come into it in the right way' (Heidegger 1962:195).

Finally, *faith* is a necessary preunderstanding if we are to 'grasp the self disclosure of God rightly' (Ferguson 1986:5). Texts may be read for linguistic data or aesthetic appreciation. However, the nature of the biblical text (which has a theological orientation) presupposes a new event of understanding as an ultimate goal of reading. When we expose ourselves to the *world of the text* we are enlarged because 'every human understanding of God is at the same time an understanding of oneself or vice-versa' (Tracy 1981:429).

Understanding should be the final objective of interpretation involving the fusion of horizons. The world of the reader fuses with the world of the text. The reader enters into it and is transformed by the world before the text and the textual world is modified by the reader's interpretation. Even then texts interpreted can be understood *truly* but not *exhaustively*.

VII A text is the work of an author(s) which is written for some purpose or function. What the text says, is what the author intends to say.[26]

Without human intent to mean something, there is no basis to look for meaning. Some argue that seeking an author's original meaning is appropriate when dealing with a living communicator but once the author dies, meaning is set free and there is no moral obligation to return to his intent. However, as Hirsch (1967:4–5) warns, speaking of literature in general that to 'banish the original author as the determiner of meaning [is] to reject the only compelling normative principle that could lend validity to an interpretation.' According to Fishbane (1979: xii) texts 'reflect not only the creative impulse of the original composers, but that of . . . revisers and arrangers as well.' Furthermore, if we totally banish the textual intention which is given in the text, we rob ourselves of a viable criterion for judging valid interpretation and open all floodgates of speculative subjectivism.

The proper object of text interpretation is not the author's intention but *world of the text*. The notion of the text implies a certain objectivity of meaning which puts a distance between the text and reader and access to this *meaning* requires distanciation and fusion.

VIII The unity of meaning can be preserved in the ancient context of the biblical text while allowing for diverse applications in modern context by maintaining a distinction between sense (meaning) and significance.[27]

Right application of the text depends on right interpretation. We need to distance ourselves from the historical situation of the text before making any application. A text should never be made to be what it never was. To bridge the gap between then and now, we need to principalize the text. In this way we can preserve textual meaning (sense) of the text and a new/different (significance) meaning in our contemporary (personal) context.[28]

This distinction has been well explained by Quinn and Erickson.

> Meaning is a property of the line of statement: Meaning is formulated, it is there in as many words; all we have to do is to recapture the rhythm that makes them meaningful. Significance is the property of the sideway expansion: significance is unformulated: what comes into existence in our minds is the result of a collaboration between the author and us. Significance is our response: it is what we make of the text.
>
> (Quinn 1992:65)

> The author's meaning is the meaning, while the application of that meaning to later audience is a question of significance. This solution serves the unity of meaning, while allowing for diversity of readers to benefit from the teaching. It is a case of one meaning, with many applications.
>
> (Erickson 1993:23)

This seemingly neglected yet vital nuance allows for the stabilisation and preservation of the textual meaning for all ages while enabling multiple and manifold applications to be made in light of present situations. The relevance of the text for each generation whose response to the text is different can be preserved without *distorting* the original message.

A text may be used differently from how its author intended to use it. It may also be used in many different ways provided we make a distinction between interpreting the text and using the text.

Another way of putting it is to say that *textual meaning* refers to the meaning of the text in light of historical context while *accommodated meaning* refers to the core of the text independent of its context (Schneiders 1991:1163).[29]

IX All texts belong to particular genres and correct identification of genre helps to produce accurate interpretation.

Biblical texts are multidimensional.[30] They are written by different people at different times in different places under different circumstances. Therefore we can expect the different types of writings being produced. The technical name given is genre.

What is a genre? It is 'a recognizable and established category of written work employing such common conventions as will prevent readers or audiences from mistaking it for another kind '(Baldick 1990:90). Genres are characterised by their adherence to a given set of fixed conventions[31] which give a necessary framework for contact with the readers. A text that bears no resemblance of structure or content cannot be understood. We need to remember that genres are 'convenient reader designed constructs that are helpful in understanding literary texts . . . they are not rigid final forms into which a writer must fit his ideas' (Woodard & Travers 1995:42).

Classification of genre can be descriptive or prescriptive. The three characteristics of a genre are form, content and intentionality (Giese 1995:11). Genres can be discerned because 'literary production is not an autonomous and self reflexive activity but rather a social and institutional event' (McGann 1983:10). Moreover, since texts are structured according to their communicative perspective, they require specific genres. Hence we must read the text according to their genres.[32] On the other hand, we need to bear in mind that the study of literary texts by genre is not an exclusive method of literary analysis but a supplement and complement of other valuable and necessary procedures (Woodard & Travers 1995:42). Hence we should not be over dogmatic in cataloguing genres.

Not all texts in the Bible are written about history. Therefore to concentrate on genres similar to modern historiography or historical categories represents a severe and unwarranted reduction. Restricting meaning to historical information or explicating meaning only with reference to historical causes artificially and narrows the base for a theological use of Scripture (Robinson 1988:150–151).

Readers who ignore the genres of the Bible do so at their own risk. Genre analysis is important because it 'helps the readers to see the similarities among various texts within a genre and the differences among various genres, thereby alerting readers to important considerations in interpretation' (Woodard & Travers 1995:36). Moreover, genre controls our reading and imaginative latitude. It tells the reader what to expect and sets up the expectation.

Vanhoozer (1995a:12) has reminded us that

> establishing a text's genre is perhaps the most important interpretive move one can make. Only when we know what kind of whole we have before us will we be able to understand the individual parts. Many misunderstandings of the Bible stem from a failure to appreciate the genre. When this happens, we make a category mistake; we read a text as if it were one thing when actually it is something quite different.

X Biblical texts are to be read like any other book which means taking the literary, linguistic and historical aspects of Scripture seriously.

Hermeneutica sacra and *hermeneutica profana* are not to be differentiated because the occasion and process of understanding in a human mind works the same way regardless of one's religious or non religious background.[33] From a theological viewpoint, the *imago dei* in every human being argues strongly for the blurring of that distinction since the *imago dei* during the Fall was not destroyed but defaced and distorted.[34] As human beings we possess the innate capacity to think and use language because of the *imago dei* (Nash 1982:119).

As Mazzeo (1978:16–17) contends:

> We cannot suspend our rational faculties or the methods of scientific inquiry whereby a text is denominated sacred. Nor can the believer in the Holy Scripture invoke divine guidance and rise up from the text with what it "really" means. The believer may find uses for the sacred text that elude the unbeliever but as the exegete he must follow the same signposts on the road to understanding.

The Meeting Point (*Anknüpfungspunkt*) between God and man through language is possible because of Incarnation.[35] This establishes a communicative link between God and man. Jesus Christ as both God and man establishes a conceptual framework whereby we can believe that God can communicate in terms understandable to human beings (Lints 1993:63). To put it in another way, 'Christ became God's epistemological grace' (Gabriel Fackre).

The speech of God has entered into the continuum of time and space which arrives 'clothed in a cultural history and addresses itself to people across cultural histories' (Lints 1993:60). Because of the Incarnation, I maintain that human language can communicate adequately and truly the knowledge of God and at the same time human can be the recipient of that cognitive word of God. Incarnation is a sufficient basis to ground the communication of truth from God to humanity. In sum, human logos can know divine logos because of the incarnation of the Logos.'[36]

XI The canonical character of Scripture requires that individual texts be treated independently and interdependently. In other words, a canonical text is to be read first of all for itself and then in the context of other canonical texts.

A canonical reading considers positioning and grouping of the various books in the canon as important. Features of arrangements in the canonical writing are not accidental but purposeful. As Sailhamer (1995:249) reasons,

> It appears that the shape of the canon was not a historical accident but rather the result of a deliberate attempt to establish certain fundamental notions about the Hebrew Bible in light of the decline of the role of prophecy and the growing importance of the written word of God as a means of determining his will.

The text must be taken together in order for the canonical force to be realized. In other words, 'it becomes necessary to see the whole of the Old Testament in the light of its canonical form as having its own stature and dignity' (Rendtorff 1993a:55). Instead of concentrating on each separate text in isolation, all books are to be considered individually and collectively.

To interpret a text canonically means we must not pit one part of Scripture against another or interpret any detail of Scripture that undermines its basic message. This does not mean we fail to appreciate the distinctiveness of various authors. It means that the canon is something given and not subjected to empirical justification by anything external to itself. What establishes the canon is the testimony of faith and not reason. While the canon is essentially a theological notion and theological confession, it does not render pluralistic readings illegitimate. Ultimately what counts is the canonical context and not the historical context of the original writer.

The process of reading a text in its canonical context can be considered a form of intertextuality.[37] Intertextuality means a network of texts in relationship to other texts. It insists that texts are not self contained nor do they function in a closed system. But rather, a text is normally filled with references, echoes or allusions. Intertexuality means a later reading of an earlier text. To consider the Bible intertextually does not mean to smother dissonant voices but to synthesize and to establish a network of similitude.

Intertextual study of biblical texts is important because texts do not exist in a vacuum. But rather, they are related to one another. Texts are only understood with reference to a framework of categories and values developed within its textual culture and particular language within which it is formed. Hence in any intertextual study, the reader must know one or more texts in order to understand a work of literature in terms of its overall significance (Riffaterre 1990:56).[38]

As Barr (1995:2) contends,

> Within the Hebrew Biblical Tradition, it is fairly common for parallel texts to be created, in which an older form has been used by a later writer or writers and has been modified by amplification, omission, alteration of wording and change of position; and that the effect of such modifications was, at least potentially, to alter the historical depiction conveyed by the text or to alter the religious and theological impression created, or both.[39]

Intertextualists would argue that there is no such thing as a self interpreting reality. Reality is understood within interpretive framework ie through the lens of the texts. The meaning of biblical texts is inexplicable apart from other texts.

The limit to applying intertextuality for certain communities of readers is the canon.[40] It does not go outside of the canon or use extra textual frame of reference for meaning. Instead, it considers 'how the texts' own use of language constitute their distinctive meaning and then use the text as an instrument through which to interpret the word' (Wood 1987:16). In a word, *Scriptura Scripturam interpretus*.[41]

Interpretation was done by community since the texts were addressed to and accepted by the community. Hence, it is not illogical to assume that although the community's interest in the texts was interpretive rather than descriptive, it did not ignore the canonical contours.

Dockery (1992:180) hits the target when he asserts,

> ultimately, the question of limits for the possible meaning of a text is determined by the canon. The canon establishes a permissible range of resignification. Although our text is an ancient document because it has a canonical shape it has an ongoing meaning and authority for the believing community.[42]

XII There are limits to the range of admissible interpretation. When a conflict of interpretation emerges, validation is necessary. Textual integrity is maintained when understanding of the text is verified by textual coherence, consistency and claims.

Anytime we read a text, it is open to a wide spectrum of interpretation. The reason is not difficult to find. Our association of ideas is subjective and different people bring different perspectives to the texts based on different past experiences. Therefore, our preference for meaning is inevitably ideologically motivated. As Newton (1986:216) remarks:

> In any subject one can invent pluralistic interpretation because one cannot exhaust analogical possibilities, associations or connotations of a text and interest can make you see connection or correct connotation.

Potentially, a text may be interpreted in several different ways, but textually not all interpretations are valid. Some are better than the others though they may be all valid from some standpoints. Nevertheless, I agree with Juhl (1980:199) that there is in principle only one correct interpretation at work and 'whatever King Lear may be about, it is not about Manchester United' (Newton 1986:212, quoting Terry Eagleton). There are certain interpretations which are preposterous in light of the context of the text. 'But, even though the interpreters cannot decide which interpretation is the privileged one, they can agree on the fact that certain interpretations are not contextually legitimated' (Eco 1990:41).

Similarly Jeanrond (1991:116) comments:

> . . . a reading that claims to have interpreted the text, yet in reality has either only interpreted a section of the text outside of its textual context or used the text or fragments of it in order only to promote the reader's own thoughts, must be considered fraudulent.

An interpreter is entitled to say that a text can mean many things but not everything because the properties of the text set the limits to the range of legitimate interpretation. A text may mean many things but not endless things; while it may have an indefinite range of possible interpretations they cannot be infinite.[43] 'Interpretation involves explaining why words can do many things and not others' (Eco 1993:24). Therefore, 'to say that a text is potentially unlimited' is not tantamount to saying that 'interpretation has no object and that it riverruns merely for its own sake.' (ibid:3–4).

Again to quote Eco (1990:21),

> A text is a place where the polysemy of symbols is in fact reduced because in a text symbols are anchored to their contexts . . . symbols are paradigmatically open to infinite meanings but syntagmatically, that is, textually open to the indefinite but by no means infinite, interpretations allowed by the context.

How can one test the validity of one's interpretation when faced with an array of different interpretive options? One approach is to use several 'objective criteria' to adjudicate among all competing interpretive frameworks. When there is a convergence of several of these 'objective criteria' (principles), then what is plausible or possible becomes most probable in the validation process. We can therefore say that the greater the convergence, the greater the viability and validity. Some of the principles that can and should be used in validation process include the following:

Principle of Coherence. When an interpreter faces some interpretive alternatives, he should choose the reading which best meets the criterion of coherence (Hirsch 1967:236–237; Eco 1990:60).[44] Or as Jeanrond (1982:6) puts it, 'validation of our reading is through the explanation of the structural organisation of the textual composition'. A valid interpretation has to be consistent with itself, that is free from internal contradiction. This is corroborated by Reichert (1977:97):

> . . . It is usually possible, when two interpretations are actually in conflict, to adjudicate between them . . . and of the two conflicting interpretations the better is the one that accounts for the words of the text more completely, simply, consistently and coherently.

Principle of Corroboration. When an interpreter has two possible interpretations, the interpretation which can best account for the greatest number of facts provided by the text and offer a better qualitative convergence between the traits is to be preferred (Hirsch 1967). The difference between a poor explanation and a good one is that the former can be said to be narrow or far fetched while the latter be said to be satisfying and covered by the principle of plenitude (ibid). As part of the corroboration, inclusiveness, intersubjectivity and efficacy can also be used (Armstrong 1990:13–19). Inclusiveness means the ability to explain all the parts without having to undergo refinements as well as to encounter anomaly and extensions. Intersubjectivity involves others regarding the interpretation to be reasonable. On the other hand, disagreement from others may signal an invalid interpretation. Efficacy means having the power to lead to new discoveries. It has also been pointed out that an interpretation can be accepted if it is confirmed [by the text as a whole] but must be rejected if it is challenged by another portion of the same text (Eco 1990:59). Thus the internal textual coherence controls the otherwise uncontrollable drives of the reader.

Principle of Institution. This refers to tradition, interpretive community and authority.[45] While contemporary literary theories are hostile to the concept of authority or institutions that claim the right to settle disputes, I agree with Newton (1986:219) that the need for authority is principally pragmatic but also biblically instituted.[46]

Principle of Intolerability of Incompatible. When there are two interpretations and both of them are logically incompatible, they cannot both be true (Beardsley 1970:44).[47] Therefore we have to choose one or the other.

Principle of Accountability. A valid interpretation should be able to account for the text as it stands, independently of other proposed interpretation. Each time an emendation has to be made in order to make the text fit the interpretation, such interpretation is questionable (Schneiders 1991:165)

Principle of Success. A valid interpretation should be able to explain anomalies in the text more successfully than its competitors and use all methods responsibly that are appropriate within the framework of interpretation (Schneiders 1991:166–167).

Principle of Least Meaning. Martin Joo's theorem is that 'the best meaning is the least meaning' (quoted by Silva 1983:153). In other words, the narrowest possible meaning is usually the correct one in individual contexts. In the light of the nature of language and communication, we should only assume one meaning unless strong exegetical (literary or contextual grounds) evidence suggest otherwise (ibid: 151).

Principle of Inadmissibility. One of the most common methods used in support of a particular theory or interpretation is the argument of silence. This type of argument must not be used. It is dangerous because it can be used to prove almost anything or support any position just like prooftexting. The silence of the text should not be equated simply with absence of textual evidence.

Principle of Then and Now. Before we can know what a text means today, we must know what it meant then. In other words, 'a text cannot mean what it never meant' (Fee and Stuart 1981: 26).

In sum, when there is an internal coherence of interpretive framework, external consistency with other established areas of knowledge, the offer of resolution of ancient problems and anomalies, the provision of illuminative power to foster new insights and areas of investigation, the accountability for the greatest number of facts/features provided by the text, then the validity of our interpretation is very much strengthened.[48]

XIII **Texts have internal and external referential function. To grasp the meaning of a text truly, we need to proceed from sense to reference i.e. from what the text as a whole says to what the text is ultimately about. Biblical texts are theologically oriented hence they demand a theological reading from the perspective of faith[49]**

Biblical texts are *linguistically* about something but *referentially* about Someone. It is rhetorically about *many* subjects but referentially about *the* Subject. While the object of interpretation is always the text, its subject is the Transcendent. Young and Ford's (1990:10) point is valid when they say

> to understand a text it is necessary to know what it refers to. The Bible does not just refer to particular events or people, or things of the past. It refers to other realities.

Earlier on, we have established that every text has a communicative function (eg legal texts to prevent crime, bereaved texts to console, etc.).[50] For biblical texts, I maintain that the communicative function is theological. While the interpretation of the text is vertically theological, it is horizontally syntactical and semantical.

A theological reading is consistent and compatible with the textual claims of the Bible. In reading the Bible, a reader gets the feeling that 'the

Bible is pervaded by a consciousness of God. It constantly interprets human experience from a religious perspective' (Ryken and Longman 1993:34). Seeing biblical texts as theological means going beyond interpreting specific texts in relation to their contexts and seeking to understand all reality as belonging to God.[51] It is only natural that a 'theological reading aims at the theological disclosure of the sense of those texts which mediate testimony of God's manifestation in the world,' (Jeanrond 1988:118).[52]

Significantly Barton (1993:6) sounds a clarion call for Old Testament study to be reunited with theology proper, reorientated towards religious faith and theological truth.[53] What a timely reminder when he says that the Old Testament is part of a volume called 'the Holy Scripture' not 'An Interesting Collection of Ancient Hebrew and Aramaic Religious Documents'.[54] Even Barr (1973b:15) concedes the theological nature of the text and eloquently opines:

> It would indeed be a thin and no doubt a useless reading of the Bible that did not recognise its profoundly religious and theological character; indeed, it is almost fantastic to suppose that one might read it without recognising that it was written not out of joy in the sonorousness of its own language, out of pleasure on its own literary quality, but because it wanted to say something about God and his words, God and his dealings with man.

In arguing for a theological reading, I am simply recognising the fact that biblical texts have a theological dimension which is *implicitly* stated though not *explicitly* expressed. This does not mean that every text belongs to a theological genre but each text must be understood on its own terms. It is also essential to recognise the multi faceted nature of biblical literature. Longman (1987:71) correctly points out that 'the danger of reading the Bible is that it radically distorts the message as it comes from the ultimate sender (God) to us as its present receivers.'

Hence what I am asserting is that the ultimate reference point of all Biblical texts is God. He is the point of all references and convergence of all other referents. The pivotal difference between biblical interpretation and other hermeneutics with regard to the text is the *Majesty* (Barth's term) of the subject matter.

Two citations by Fishbane (1989:35) and Lewis (1961:32–33) will further sustain my arguments.

> . . . Hebrew Scripture is an ontologically unique literature: not because of its aesthetic style or topics of concern—which are judged weak in comparison with contemporary medieval romances and epics—but precisely because such externalities are merely the first of several garments—like layers concealing deeper

and less—refracted aspects of divine truth whose love, the root of all roots, is God himself.

The Bible is through and through, a sacred book. Most of its component parts were written, and all of them were brought together, for a purely religious purpose. Not only is it a sacred book but a book so remorselessly and continuously sacred that it does not invite, it excludes or repels, the merely aesthetic approach.

The question then arises 'since biblical texts are theologically oriented, is a non theological reading possible and permissible?' In my opinion, the answer is yes because it can be done from the 'point of view of the technique of reading but it may not lay claim to finally do justice to the text' (Jeanrond 1988:127). The issue in reading biblical text is not so much as whether the reader should be a believer or not. Rather the crux of the matter is that the reader 'should allow the text to validate its claim which is finally a theological claim '(Jeanrond 1988:127).

Stuhlmacher (1979:89) establishes that

in exegesis there must be an openness to an encounter with the truth of God coming to us from out of transcendence. We have expressly demanded of a hermeneutics of consent that it be open to the language of transcendence. Whoever refuses this openness . . . can interpret the historical tradition only in a very fragmentary way. . . The hermeneutical principle underlying interpretation of texts must be an openness of the possibility of faith.

Morgan and Barton (1989:274) underscore an important point when they say 'anyone who uses the bible as scripture is involved in theological interpretation consciously or unconsciously.' Hence, it is of utmost importance that we 'reflect on the process and assumptions of the theological text interpretation in a fundamental way' (Jeanrond (1988:2–3). Because biblical texts are theologically oriented, interpretation should be carried out from the perspective of faith. When biblical texts are read through the lens of faith, the horizon of the text and interpreter will fuse, providing the reader with a provocative and transformative experience.

According to Jeanrond,[55] a theological reading has several important hermeneutical implications :

- Theology is mediated by oral and written texts
- The historical revelation of God in Jesus Christ has taken on text character to the extent that human beings have linguistically borne witness to it and handed it down.
- Christian tradition consists of several collection of texts and the canonical text collections of Old and New Testament take precedence.

- Texts spur on the faith community which reads them to the disclosure of the truth of Christian faith.
- To refuse to consider the primacy of textual understanding would mean to expose oneself right from the beginning to the possibility of denying the importance of that which constitutes the sustaining sources of christian theological thought, namely the text.
- Theological texts ought to provoke theological thinking and theology is a science.
- The divine revelation of Jesus Christ is mediated through the Biblical Texts and the texts of Christian tradition because only through the textual witness can we have access to the event and person of Jesus Christ.
- In these texts a reality imposes upon us which shatters our self understanding.
- Our perspectives can only change if we are willing to expose them to such change.[56]

Notes

1   A good analogy for a text-centred approach to interpretation is to be likened to safe cracking. A safe cracker does not need to know the make of the safe; the year it was manufactured; neither the texture nor origin of the safe. All he needs to open the safe is the secret combination of the codes.

2   Cf. 'Every theory of interpretation postulates a theory of text,' echoes Jeanrond (1988:73). See Eagleton (1990:24–38) on the philosophical and sociological significance of theories.

3   My textual theory is influenced by literary theories and informed by linguistics with historico-grammatical underpinnings in dialogue with other disciplines. Acknowledgement and appropriation of insights from literary theories do not necessarily reflect a *carte blanche* approval of them. I adopt a more conservative textual approach. It is to be noted that this approach does not ignore original language, cultural settings and text critical information. It simply brackets historical questions.

Helpful discussion on textual theories can be found in Wolfgang U. Dressler (ed), *Current Trends in Textlinguistics* (Berlin: Walter de Gruyter, 1978); Janos S. Petofi (ed), *Text vs Sentence: Basic Questions of Text Linguistics, Part 1* (Hamburg:Helmut Buske, 1979) and Andrew Bennett, *Readers and Reading* (England: Longman, 1995).

4   In addition to others, two works of Umberto Eco's *The Limits to Interpretation* (1990) and *Interpretation and Overinterpretation* (1992) are of important and relevant.

5   Central to the concept of theory is meaning. My understanding of meaning gravitates towards a realist's view rather than that of an idealist. A realist sees the text as having a separate existence, independent of the interpreter whose task is to discover it. An idealist, however denies the reality of an external world except for his own perception and cognition.

6   See also Bonycastle (1991:9).

7   Contrast Steven Knapp and Walter Benn Michaels, 'Against Theory', in W. J. T. Mitchell (ed), *Against Theory: Literary Studies and the New Pragmatism* (Chicago: The University of Chicago Press, 1985): 11–30 and Susan Sontag, *Against Interpretation* (New York: Anchor Books, Doubleday, 1961):3–14. She claims that 'to interpret is to impoverish, to deplete the world—in order to set up a shadow world of "meaning" . . .' (7). However, the weighty statement of Lentricchias quoted by Atkins and Morrow (1989:10) carries clout:

> To be against theory is to be against self examination—against raising and exploring questions about how texts and selves and societies are formed and maintained and for whose benefits. To be against theory is to take everything at face value and never to be suspicious.

8   Our definition is influenced by Crystal (1992:72). Linguistically speaking, the word text can refer to any passage, spoken or written of whatever length that forms a unified whole (Halliday & Hasan 1976:1). See also Fowler (1986:53–68) on how texts are made.

9   Consider the definition given by Yury M. Lotman in 'The Text within the Text', in *Publications of the Modern Language Association of America* 109/3:377–384. His definition of a text is 'a mechanism constituting a system of heterogeneous semiotic spaces, in whose continuum the message [associated with the first textual function] circulates'.
       Such a definition is so profound that it leaves me flabbergasted!
       See also Ruqaiya Hasan 'The Texture of a Text,' in David Graddol & Oliver Boyd-Barrett, *Media Texts: Authors and Readers* (Clevendon, England: Multilingual Matters Ltd, 1994):74–160

10   The words *text* and *discourse* are used synonymously. A discourse / textual analysis refers to the study of the actual wording of a written text and how the sentences relate to one another coherently. Linguistically, since a text comprises a number of sentences, it belongs to the category of discourse of which a sentence is a base unit. Thus, to establish the meaning of a text is to establish meaning fixed on the sentences.

11   According to Ricoeur (1976:22–44), three changes takes place when a speech divine is fixed into writing:

       1) A text becomes semantically autonomous to the intention of the written. The text has its own meaning regardless of what the author intended.
       2) A written text is cut loose from the socio-cultural context of composition. A first century text written to Romans does not have to be as if we are Romans. The meaning of a text is not limited to its original context.
       3) A text is emancipated from ostensive reference. The text's original reference to particular reasons, things, events in context shared by speaker and hearer is no longer determinative of a text's meaning.

       For more details, see his book, *Interpretation Theory: Discussion and Surplus of Meaning* (Fort Worth Tx: Texas Christian University 1976).

12   According to van Dijk (1972), a sentence differs from a text in that the former is a unit of grammar, a static unit of language, can only be described by breaking into constituents or elements while the former has a communicative function, dynamic process of communication and has a holistic character (132–175).

13   A similar observation is made by Barr (1973a:178).

14   A sentence is a syntactic unit whose syntax (ordering of words and phrases) is semantically based. Its function is to make meaning tangible as signs arranged in space (writing) or time (space). The core meaning is the propositions (Fowler 1986:69).
       According to Vanhoozer, every sentence has 1) a proposition—about something; 2) purpose—it functions to fulfil; 3) presence—it expresses a purpose in a particular form (presence) which indicates direction; and 4) power—it possesses power to accomplish its task.

For more details, see Kevin Vahoozer, 'The Semantics of Biblical Literature', in *Hermeneutics, Authority and Canon*, ed. D A Carson & John Woodbridge (Grand Rapids: Zondervan 1986):52–104.

15   There are five types of cohesion: reference, substitution, ellipsis, conjunction and lexical cohesion. See Halliday and Hasan (1976).

16   See Noble (1991): 120–121.

17   Ferdinand de Saussure, the father of modern linguistics differentiates between language as *Langue* (system) and *Parole* (always synchronic). *Langue* is the linguistic code with specific structure and *Parole* is the actualization of linguistic codes. The former is a system, the latter is an event.

18   Cf. Crystal's (1992:82) definition: 'The parts of an utterance next to or near a linguistic unit (such as a word) which is the focus of attention . . . without knowing the context, the meaning of a word is likely to be ambiguous . . .'

19   While a historical critical method endeavours to discover the compositional history of the text, the textual approach is more interested in the compositional techniques of the narrator. In other words, it is referential function versus poetic function. The two approaches have been described metaphorically as a *window* and a *mirror*. The historical critic sees the text as a window through which he learns about events of another place, time, etc, while the literary critic sees the text as a mirror in which whatever insights obtained is the result of an encounter between the interpreter and the text itself.

20   Scribal glosses, addenda must be preserved as authentic and in their own rights since they have great analytical potential of serving as indices to the textual and theological revision. See Fishbane (1989:42).

21   In other words, a text is presumed to be innocently holistic unless proven guilty otherwise!

22   Cf the statement of Morgan & Barton (1989:7) 'What is decisive is not the claim of the text but aim and interest of the interpreters.' Although they also add that all aims are legitimate but not all are equally appropriate (ibid: 236).

23   Cf. Ebeling's dictum : From understanding "of" a language to understanding through language." See Gerhard Ebeling, *Word of God and Hermeneutics*, trans. James W Leitch (Philadelphia: Fortress Press 1963): 318.

24   Cf. Tracy (1981:59) who remarks 'a theologian (interpreter) should render explicit his/her method of interpretation. Included in that explication should be arguments defending any claim that the general rules of interpretation may have to be changed in order to interpret religious texts or events.'

25   Cf. Morgan & Barton 1989:257 who reminds us that

Methodological foundation must be spelt out because they are based upon certain philosophical and theological assumptions. Assumptions make a difference how we understand a text. Though the written text may be fixed, the reader brings some preunderstanding, some aims, interests and this affects the way the text is read.

For a good discussion of how one's philosophical commitment affects one's approach to interpretation, see Royce Gordon Gruenler, *Meaning and Understanding: The Philosophical Framework for Biblical Interpretation* (FCI vol 2; Grand Rapids: Zondervan, 1991).

26   While acknowledging the fact that once a work is published, it has semantic autonomy from the author and that meaning of the text lies in the constitutive elements in the texts like sentences, words, etc., we are not prepared to dismiss the relevance of the author in the comprehension of the text. As Eco (1993:16) puts it,

> We have to respect the text, not the author as person so and so. Nevertheless, it can look rather crude to eliminate the poor author as something irrelevant from the story of an interpretation.

From another standpoint, in certain kinds of writing eg love letter or especially in a will, it is relevant and imperative to know the author and his intention. I submit that Scripture is a *theological will* (Old and New Testament) drafted by authors (solicitors) whose testator is the *Author* (God).

27   E D Hirsch Jr., is one of the primary advocates of this distinction. See Hirsch (1967).

28   Instead of meaning and significance, a clearer term to use is *sense* and *significance* or *signification* and *significance*. See Morris (1964) for his work on signification and significance in: *A Study of the Relations of Signs and Values* (Cambridge, Mass.: MIT, 1964).
        As Erikson (1993:59) puts it, 'signification is the dimension of meaning with respect to the relationship between a sign or term and that which it signifies. Significance refers to the dimension of meaning with respect to the relationship between the sign and someone knowing it.'
        Oey has also suggested a distinction be made between what the text says (historical context) and what the text means (contemporary context) in a personal conversation with the author.

29   For issues pertaining to contextualisation, see John M. Hitchin, 'Culture and the Bible: The Question of Contextualisation', *Melanesian Journal of Theology* 8:2 (1992):30–52; Daniel Smith-Christopher, *Text and Experience: Toward a Cultural Exegesis of the Bible* (England: Sheffield, 1995); L. C. Jonker, 'Bridging the Gap between Bible Readers and "Professional" Exegetes', *Old Testament Essays* 10:1 (1997):69–83; L. C. Jonker, 'On Plotting the Exegetical-Hermeneutical Landscape', *Scriptural Journal of Biblical Studies* 59:4 (1996):397–411; Fernando F. Segovia, and Mary Ann Tolbert (eds), *Readings From This Place: I Social Location and Biblical Interpretation in the United States* (Minneapolis: Fortress Press, 1995) and Gerald West and Musa W. Dube (eds), *'Reading With': An Exploration of the Interface Between Critical and Ordinary Readings of the Bible: African Overtures* (Semeia 73; Atlanta: Scholars Press, 1996).

30   Incidentally, a literary approach seems to do better justice to the diversity of genres found in the text.

31   Conventions include some established practices such as techniques, styles, structures that are commonly adopted by writers which are implicitly if not explicitly agreed upon. Some examples are dramas, novels, poetry, science fiction, etc. Thus, to read a story book as if it were a legal document is simply to misread it.

32   In a similar vein Corti (1978:115) affirms:

> Texts do not exist in isolation usually because they are a sign function, it belongs with other signs to a group, to a literary genre. Genre serves as the place where the individual work enters into a complex network of relations with other works. See also the long discussion by Longman (1987:75–100).

33   At the same time I also recognise that there are some differences between the principles of *hermeneutica profana* and *hermeneutica sacra*. For the latter, there are some priniciples which are unique only to it. As Roland Chia has remarked that once a decision (ie, a theological decision made by faith) is made on the nature of the text in question, the approach of the reader to the text will be different and will also be governed by a different hermeneutic (in a written correspondence with the author).

34   A common understanding among the main stream of Christianity.

35   I want to thank Professor Auld for this insight.
     For a defence of a logical coherence of Incarnation, see John S. Feinberg, 'The Incarnation of Christ', in Douglas Geivett and Gary Habermas (eds), *In Defense of Miracles* (Downers Grove, Illinois: Intervarsity Press, 1997): 226–246; Thomas V. Morris, *The Logic of God Incarnate* (Ithaca, NY: Cornell University press, 1986).
     See also the excellent article of Ford Lewis Battles, 'God was Accommodating Himself to Human Capacity,' *Interpreters* vol 31 (Jan 1977) 19–38 and C. Stephen Evan, *The Historical Christ and the Jesus of Faith: The Incarnational Nature of Christianity* (Oxford: Clarendon Press, 1996).
     For a contrasting view, see John Hick, *The Metaphor of God Incarnate: Christology in a Pluralistic Age* (London: SCM, 1994).

36   Contra contemporary theologians who declare that cognitive knowledge of God is impossible. Revelation is not God giving us information by communication but we receive communion through personal encounter. See John Baillie, *The Idea of Revelation in Recent Thought* (NY: Columbia University Press, 1956) 29.
     Such theological agnosticism (represented by Brunner, Tillich, Bultmann, Temple, Baillie) is to be rejected. Instead, the traditional view that human beings have the ability to know the Transcendent God through propositions is to be preferred. Human language is capable of serving as an *adequate* though not complete carrier of information about God. When we try to separate the experience of God from the cognitive knowledge of God we are creating a false dichotomy of God because 'He is not silent but He has spoken' (Schaeffer's phrase).

> Our knowledge of God is always partial, but it is none the less authentic because it is inseparably linked to the divine disclosure and the fact that we

have been created in the image of God. When God speaks, He can be understood by the divine image bearers (Lints 1993:64).

37   Intertextuality seeks to demonstrate relationships between texts and is to be viewed as a phenomenon where one original text (genotext) is imported into another later text (phenotext). This implies that a reader who does not know any other text cannot identify its intertextual relationships. How the text came into being (production) is not as important as the final text product which is compared with other texts in synchronic relationships.

There are two forms of marked intertextuality. An intentional iconicity based on ungrammaticality or explicit allusions to other texts in the phenotext (later text) eg OT quotations in NT or Torah in the prophets. They may be regarded as forms of marked and intended intertextuality.

The other is 'unintentional iconicity where the reader explains the syntagmatic ordering in the ungrammaticalities of the text by positing an analogous connection with elements in another texts' (van Wolde 1994:183).

A diachronic intertextual analysis investigates the unmarked intertextemes-genre, code etc. while a synchronic intertextual analysis investigates the functioning of a genotext in a phenotext on the basis of marked textual relationships, which are in part dependent on the iconization of the reader.

My use of the word 'intertextual' has a more limited meaning than the current use of the word in literary circle.

For a concise understanding of intertextuality's modern usage in literary criticism and its critique, see Ellen van Wolde, *Words Become Worlds: Semantic Studies of Genesis 1–11* (Leiden: E. J. Brill, 1994): 160–199 but especially 161–165. See also Gerrie Synyman, 'Who is Speaking? Intertextuality and Textual Influence', *Neotestamentica* 30: 2 (1996):427–449; George Aichele and Gary Phillips (eds), *Intertextuality and the Bible* (Semeia 67/70; Atlanta: Scholars Press, 1995 [1996]) and George Wesley Buchanan, *Introduction to Intertextuality* (Mellen Biblical Press Series, 26; Lewiston-Queenston-Lampeter: Edwin Mellen, 1994).

38   Another related term is inner biblical exegesis popularised by Fishbane (1985). Essentially, it is reusing, reinterpreting and reapplying earlier biblical material within the OT itself. Some of the ways to detect such method used is the appearance of glosses, arrangement of material in the present form, direct quotes, reusing of earlier themes and traditions.

There are some inherent difficulties with this approach. One is subjectivity. What is considered an allusion by one may not be that clear to someone else. The problem is compounded since we do not know much about the process by which biblical material was written down, the sources used and what was available to different people. Added to that, it is not always easy to know when two passages coincide, whether resemblance between two texts is coincidental, who is borrowing from whom, or when both have a common source. Hence, the danger of specifying the process of the author's citation.

39   Taken from Introduction to the second edition in Allan Barr's *A Diagram of Synoptic Relationships* (Edinburgh: T&T Clark, 1995, rep 1938).

40   See also Elmer Dycke, 'Canon As Context For Interpretation' , in Elmer Dycke (ed), *The Act of Reading Bible* (UK Paternoster Press, 1996):33–64.

41   Intertextual study is enjoying a wide currency today. Such terms as textual/intertextual/intratextual/extratextual are used. Intertextuality 'designates the way in which a body of scripture (biblical texts) serves as an interpretive medium for its component parts, while intratextuality, designates the way in which the same body of scripture serves' (Riffaterre 1990:56).

      The main difference between the trinity of texts (textual, intratextaul and intertextual) and extratextual is this: The former, do not reconstruct symbolic system of ancient authors. Instead they seek to grasp the meaning of the text in themselves. Whereas the latter seeks to locates primary realities outside any particular interpretative scheme (ie canonical texts).

      Other terms used in intertextual study are architext, transtextuality, paratextuality, metatextuality, etc.

42   For a good example of an intertextual study between Exodus 17:1–7 and Numbers 20:1–13, consult Lim (1997):134–154.

43   There is a need to recognise, 'infinity of interpretation with univocality of the message', says Eco (1990:12). It is interesting to note that Eco has shifted his position from admissible infinite range of interpretation to a limit on pluralism.

44   It needs to be pointed out that according to Hirsch, verification by the criterion of coherence depends on reconstruction of the author's outlook.

45   Johann Cook has argued that there must be an interplay of Text and Tradition if we want to arrive at the ultimate intention of the authors/redactors. See, his article on ' Text and Tradition: A Methodological Problem', *Journal of Northwest Semitic Languages* 9 (1981):3–11.

46   Nevertheless, I contend that the final court of appeal for correct interpretation is the institution of Textuality comprising three chief Justices (Text, Intratext and Intertext).

      In my exegetical explication of an enigmatic episode in Numbers 20:1–13, this is the route I took to solve the Pentateuchal Puzzle which in my judgement has proven to be satisfactory.

      An important principle to bear in mind in any exegesis is that, any exegetical answer given by an exegete should be exegetically decided on textual ground. In exegesis, I ask a few basic but very important questions.

      1. Is the explanation plausible?
      2. If it is, what is the degree of plausibility?
      3. Is this the most satisfactory reading of the (con)text?
      4. Is this reading most sensitive to the (con)text?
      5. Is this reading textually demonstrable?
      6. Does this reading disturb the (con)text the least?
      7. Does it make the best sense in the light of other texts?

Consult my monograph (1997) for details and application.

47   This does not deny that ambiguity does exist in some cases where we cannot be sure of correct interpretation. Ambiguity can be the result of the writer's intention or because of our imperfect knowledge.

48   It has also been suggested that the scale of 0 to 1 be used for resolving paradoxes of self referentiality. If the value is 0.5, it is more or less probable.

49   The general orientation of this section owes much to two very significant books by Jeanrond—*Theological Hermeneutics : Development and Significance* (1991) and *Text and Interpretation as Categories of Theological Thinking* (1988).

50   Cf. 'A text is not written for its own sake but rather to function within a particular aim in mind in the real world' (van Wolde 1994:181).

51   Cf. Ricoeur's dictum: 'Not what is said, but about what it is said.'

52   For a persuasive exposition of the theological nature of Biblical texts, see Lints (1993:259–289) especially 287–288 on redemption matrix. See also Dunn (1977).

53   Interestingly, this call was made at his inaugural lecture as the Oriel and Laing Professor of the Interpretation of Holy Scripture at Oxford in 1992.

54   A fact which biblical scholars often times ignore or forget!

55   See pages 7–8; 74; 150–151.

56   For a helpful introduction to some theological issues see, Claude Geffre and Werner Jeanrond, *Why Theology?* (Concilium; London: SCM, 1994); John Reumann (ed), *The Promise and Practice of Biblical Theology* (Minneapolis: Fortress Press, 1991); Schubert M. Ogden, *Doing Theology Today* (Valley Forge, Pennsylvania: Trinity Press International, 1996); Schubert M. Ogden, 'Theology and Biblical Interpretation' *Journal of Religion* 76:2 (1996):172–188; Brian D. Ingrafia, *Postmodern Theory and Biblical Theology* (Cambridge: Cambridge University Press, 1996); Paul Badham, 'What is Theology?' *Theology* 99:78 (1996):101–106; Stephen E. Fowl (ed), *The Theological Interpretation of Scripture: Classic and Contemporary Readings* (Oxford: Blackwell Publishers, 1997) and; Henry T. C. Sun and Keith L. Eades (eds), *Problems in Biblical Theology: Essays in Honor of Rolf Knierim* (Grand Rapids: Eerdmans, 1997); Gerald O' Collins and Daniel Kendall, *The Bible for Theology: Ten Principles for the Theological Use of Scripture* (Paulist, 1997) and a series of excellent articles in *Biblical Interpretation* 6/2 (1998):131–257.
      In a helpful way, Klein, Bloomberg and Hubbard (1993:377–399) suggest the following practical use of theology:

      1) Valid theologizing must follow exegesis of biblical texts.
      2) Theology must be based on the Bible's total teaching, not on selected texts.
      3) Legitimate theologizing considers and expresses the Bible's own emphases.
      4) Theological points must be stated in ways that explain and illuminate their significance for the life and ministry of the Church today.
      5) Theology must be centred on what God has revealed.

Chapter Six

Understanding the Text

All solid knowledge and judicious defence of divine truth, must originate from a right understanding and accurate interpretation of the Scriptures. The purity of the christian religion has shone brighter or been obscured in proportion as the study of sacred interpretation has flourished or decayed (Ernesti 1824:1)

6.1 Old Testament

To read the Old Testament as a text means to take the final form of the text seriously,[1] to exegete it as a text and to understand it as a text. It bears repeating that the 'earlier stages of the text should always be interpreted as pew-stages of the text, but not as "texts" themselves. The "text can only be what we have before us in its final shape' (Rendtorff 1997:24–25). A text oriented (immanent) approach[2] to Old Testament attempts to understand the text from within in light of other texts within the canon. Each text forms a unit of meaning complete in itself. This means that meaning can be found within a textual unit in a text (a passage), intratextual (within a book or books classified by a broad category eg Pentateuch) and intertextual (the canon).

The Old Testament is the medium through which the speaker (God) communicates to men. It is the embodiment of a message which has a communicative function. The form or shape of the text is inseparable from the content (Fishbane 1979:xi) and can play an important role in determining the meaning of the text since form and content are inextricably interrelated.[3]

As a document, it is written primarily in Hebrew using literary conventions in the ancient semitic world. It is a structured piece of literary work and its meaning is governed and given by and through a network of relationships between the various elements. As a structured piece of literary work, it is a compilation of books intelligently collated for a specific purpose according to some "compositional conventions" (Fishbane's phrase). In other words, the Old Testament is not compiled haphazardly, but rather it follows some type of strategies. As Rendtorff (1991:129) points out,

> . . . compilation or composition of the Old Testament was the result of a long process where material was handed down collected and collated and worked over and given its final form. In its final form some books are self contained independent literary entities (Job, Psalms, etc) while from some books we must take into account its larger context (eg Pentateuch). The OT Text as a whole shows signs of an overall coherence and in the final composition is a meaningful text. They are at work which helps bring texts together.

The motivation for the compilation or formation of the Old testament seems to stem from theological concerns. Rendtorff (1991:126) maintains that

> in all the cases (ie formation of the OT) it is evident that the editing is not only literary but at the same time theological. The editors or authors of the larger works have a clearly recognizable theological purpose. They set their work in a particular theological perspective and give it a form through the entirety of which it makes particular theological statements. This is evidently the decisive purpose of the authors.

6.2 Received or Reconstructed Text?

One of the early assumptions in historical criticism has been that the earlier and older a text is, the more original and therefore a better text. Conversely, what is later is relegated as secondary or redactional. Thus effort has been made to reconstruct the so called Urtext, a mistaken assumption seriously challenged by scholars. As Rendtorff (1991:129) contends that

> the final form of the text provides a better foundation for exegetical activities since we have the text before us rather than a reconstructed text that is somewhat uncertain and difficult to reconstruct. It provides a hermeneutical key to correct interpretation since the final form has been the canon of scripture as authoritative for the community of believers.

6.2.1 Manuscripts
For practical reasons the Codex Leningradensis B19A (about 1009 CE) known to have been corrected according to a Ben Asher manuscript.[4] This is used as the base text in BH/BHS because it has all the books of the Bible and is considered close to the Ben Asher tradition.[5]

The Aleppo Codex (925 CE) written by Shelomo Ben Buya'a (conso-
nants only) in terms of dating and quality is to be preferred because it is a
Ben Asher Text. It is also believed to have been used by Maimonides who
is considered to be authoritative. However, it is an incomplete text because most of the Pentateuchal passages are missing, including a few
chapters from second Kings, Jeremiah, Minor prophets, Chronicles and
Psalms, as well as the final part of the codex which contains much of the
Song of Songs, Lamentations, Esther, Daniel, Ezra and Nehemiah. The
question is then asked, how reliable is the Masoretic text in light of its late
date?

According to Tov (1992:23),

> The principal component of the MT is that of the consonants (letters), evidenced
> in the Second Temple sources . . . Therefore, although the medieval form of
> MT is relatively late, its consonantal framework reflects an ancient tradition that
> was in existence more than a thousand years earlier in many sources, among
> them, many texts from the Judean desert.

He has also remarked that the combined evidence of texts from Qumran,
Masada and reconstructed Hebrew source of several Targumim and early
revision of the LXX, *kaige*-Theodotion show that the consonantal framework of the MT did not change much in the course of more than one
thousand years (ibid:30).

Similarly, Lawrence H. Schiffman in his book, *Reclaiming the Dead
Sea Scrolls* (1994) has made the claims that the copyists of the Biblical
Dead Sea Scrolls had a definite preference for the proto-Masoretic genre.
According to him not only are the 60% of the Biblical manuscripts found
in the caves proto-Masoretic but also the 20% (they represent a text
that is derived ultimately from a proto masoretic type text) which Tov
classifies as belonging to the peculiar Qumran style bringing the total
proto-Masoretic score to 80%.[6] Emanuel Tov (1995:101) gives the statis-
tics of the 84–89 Texts: he has studied some 40% of the Qumran Texts
reflect the tradition of MT with regard to orthography and content, though
not in paragraphing, while 60% are of different nature. Out of the 60%,
25% reflect Qumran orthography, 10% are close to the LXX and Samaritan versions, while 25% are non aligned texts. Thus Tov (1995:102) points
out that 'within the textual jungle, the majority of the texts belonged to
textual groups or blocks, and with these groups MT formed the largest
one.'

Therefore, there is good reason to use the MT (Codex L) as the base
text for exegesis. 'The MT is the best Hebrew representative of one of the
texts that was current in the fourth-third century,' says Tov (1981:184).

Millard (1982:152) also holds the view that 'the Dead Sea Scrolls make explicit what had previously been supposed by many, that the Masoretic text preserves an earlier text-type current in the century or so prior to the fall of Jerusalem.'

Ideally, the biblical manuscripts from the Dead Sea should be used as base texts since they predate the MT about 1000 years. Some of them were circulated as early as third century BCE. However, because the 200 or more biblical manuscripts are fragmentary in nature and there are no complete books their practicality is limited.[7]

The findings of a diversity of textual traditions of biblical manuscripts has led scholars to believe that the Qumran community (founded about 150 BCE) had no canon (of included and excluded books)[8] of the Old Testament in the sense of a defined number of sacred writings as later Rabbinic Judaism later came to have. They did not even have a standardised text. Ulrich (1984a:92) states that 'the Scriptures were pluriform (as was Judaism and Christianity) until at least 70 CE, probably until 100, and quite possibly as late as 135 or beyond.' Collins (1995:22) is probably correct when he suggests

> . . . the Qumran sect accepted some authoritative writings that were not ac-cepted elsewhere (eg books such as Enoch and Jubilees are preserved in multiple copies whereas Chronicles is barely attested and Esther is absent from the li-brary), they also share with their contemporary Jews a set of scriptures which included the Torah, prophetic writings and Psalms.

We have a textual variety resembling the consonantal text of the MT, Septuagint and Samaritan Pentateuch and other biblical writings which cannot be classified under any of the three textual traditions. Tov (1992) classifies it as Proto-Masoretic, Septuagint, Pre-Samaritan and non aligned texts (independent texts that do not stand in any specifically close rela-tionship to the MT, LXX and Samaritan group because they contain many readings not found in any of them). Although it must be said that among the texts not written in Qumran practice, the largest corpus is the MT reflecting more or less the orthography and content of the medieval bib-lical manuscripts (Tov 1995:88). However, manuscripts discovered in Masada or caves in Wadi Murabba'at have more resemblance to the con-sonantal text of the MT and do not give evidence of a pluriform textual tradition of the Old Testament as found in Qumran. The question is, how and why was the uniform textual tradition established- the tradition that underlies the medieval manuscript on which our Bibles are based?

One school of thought according to Sarna (1987:162) assumes that the text was stabilised in the second half of the century after the first Jewish revolt. Out of the destruction of Jerusalem in 70 CE, the Pharisees and scribes establish the canon of sacred scripture.[9]

Sarna postulates that the very concept of a sacred canon of Scripture by which Jewish communities established their identity, and the public reading, studying and liturgy would eventually lead to a stabilization of normative text. Assuming it is a pre-masoretic text, it would be favoured by scholarly and hierarchical circles in the Second Temple period. A uniform text would serve as a cohesive force in light of the destruction of the destruction of the Temple and the Jewish Diaspora. It is natural to assume that scribes would only copy the so called official text and all others would be discarded. Moreover, since many of the texts were written on perishable material, they would perish—except for those in the Judean desert.

On the other hand, Moshe Greenberg (1956:157–167) has argued that the text was stabilised at an earlier period due to the initiative of the scribes within the Jerusalem Temple. They made a critical selection of the various manuscripts and textual traditions and the proto- Samaritan Pentateuch and the Hebrew Text of the Septuagint during the second century BCE. This is also the view of Tov (1981) who says that 'the MT did not develop during the first two centuries of the Common Era but had already existed in the last two centuries before that beginning. It needs to be borne in mind that the texts in the Judean desert are younger than those in Qumran.'

According to van der Woude (1995:44–45), the theory of Greenberg can be supported by the discoveries at Masada of biblical writings that are proto-Masoretic, so called normative mainstream Judaism rejected the textual tradition of the Septuagint at a very early age (an example of a Greek manuscript of the Minor prophets found in Nahal Hever about 1st century BCE is a revision of the Septuagint Tradition on the basis of a Hebrew Text shows marks of similarities with the proto-Masoretic tradition that became current after 70 CE. Thus the Hebrew Vorlage of the Septuagint version was brought into conformity with the proto-Masoretic text. These Greek revisions toward the proto-Masoretic which began quite early were intended to harmonise the Greek text of the Septuagint with the proto-Masoretic tradition that was already standard in Jerusalem.[10]

At Qumran what we have are some variant manuscripts that have survived when the Hebrew Bible was being canonised by the scribes and priests in Jerusalem. The question is, how faithful is the MT to its Vorlage and trustworthy? What is the significant implication of all this?

According to van der Woulde (1995:45),

> . . . the Text of the Old Testament passed down to us is a basically faithful representation of the tradition by the spiritual leaders of early Judaism before the Roman destruction of the temple . . . we should have a great respect for this tradition, with all the consequences this has for our text critical work on the Hebrew Bible.[11]

Similarly, according to Martin Jan Mulder (1988:104) what we call the *Masoretic Text* appears to have been a Hebrew text which was authoritative in many respects and whose transmission was surrounded with great care in the Jewish world, even in sectarian groups, several centuries before the coming of the Common Era' and thus also several centuries before the activities of the actual Masoretes.

It is possible alongside the proto-masoretic texts, existed other texts that were authoritative in certain circle but diverging from the MT that had become 'official' eg Qumran. Perhaps the LXX translators (some) might have used such divergent texts as their Hebrew Vorlage. The writing of the Masora (length and number of pericopes, words, vowel, accentuation) eventually brought stabilization and standardization of the text.

6.2.2 Reliability of the Masoretes

Concerning the reliability and the role of the Masoretes,[12] we summarise Barr's theses from his *tour de force* book, *Comparative Philology* (1968:194-222). In my assessment his positon is fairly balanced and should serve as a corrective to three inaccurate views.

1) The vocalisation of the Hebrew Bible was invented only when the written marks of vocalisation were invented. This is inaccurate. While the Tiberian pointing system was invented in sixth century CE, prior to that some letters were used as vowels (*matres lectionis*). No books could have been read without vowels! The Masoretes did not invent vocalization but marks for vocalisation which was in use. A distinction needs to be made between actual existence of vocalisation and its written markings (195).

2) The predilection of the Masoretes to iron out textual and semantic difficulties. Hence they pointed the text by guessing and vocalising its meaning. This does not appear to be so. The difficulty of the existing text tends at many points to suggest that the Masoretes transmitted a received text with its own difficulties, rather than iron these out into something which by their then knowledge was smooth and satisfactory (205).

Moreover, such a view is difficult to sustain since one would have expected a primarily semantic sifting and cataloguing of material (205). However, if that was so, they would have made texts clearer!

Another factor to consider as Barr points out is that if their work involved innovation at the level of meaning, how did they succeed in getting it accepted by the religious community in view of the inertia of religious traditions and practices? How could it be carried through in midst of the Qaraintes and Rabbabites? How could the opposite party not fail to point out the wilful alteration in the vocalisation? Thus the fact of standardization of the grammatical system, if it is a fact, does not in itself justify the conception of an arbitrary moulding of the text by the Masoretes on the morphic-semantic level (206).

3) The pointing by the Masoretes can be easily ignored or dismissed. Such a flippant and facile attitude is to be discouraged. The Masoretes' pointing was recording a tradition of reading (209). Where wrong readings of the texts have grown up, we should not attribute them to the ignorance of the late Masoretes but to a much earlier stage in the tradition (before CE 2). While traditional vocalisation is subject to error, there is no evidence, however, that entitles us to carry this so far that we begin to regard the vocalisation as entirely arbitrary or chaotic and therefore subject to alteration no greater basis than the liking of the modern scholar. The vocalization is historical evidence just as other aspects of the texts are; it has to be explained and not merely altered (221).[13]

Similarly, Sailhamer (1995:204–206) has reminded us that modern readers of ancient biblical texts must rely on the vowels and accents supplied by the Masoretes. The fact they are secondary does not diminish their importance since they are the text of Scripture.

Sawyer (1972:14) also has an axe to grind with the textual critics and comparative philologists because on several occasions they have blinded us to the plain sense of the text as it stands. More often than not, passages which are quite intelligible and which made perfectly good sense to Masoretic scholars are described as difficult or impossible or meaningless as they stand. He leaves no doubt that some of the so called 'difficulties' are due to our imperfect knowledge of the ancient Near East; others to a conflict between what we know and what the text says; an inadequate knowledge of Hebrew grammar and others due to masoretic or earlier Jewish scholarly invention. His conclusion is that it is only very rarely that the masoretic text is meaningless.

Millard (1982:153) also adds his voice by saying:

. . . we freely underate the ability and the accuracy of those copyists to whom we owe the Old Testament and there is no doubt that errors were committed by copyists and have passed into the printed text. However, the modern reader's readiness to detect them should not be greater than his readiness to admit that ancient scribes and copyists could also be as precise and careful as he and may have known their business better than he. The ancient scribes deserve our thanks and praise.[14]

Notes

1   My understanding of the final form of the text makes room for textual criticism since there is bound to be copyists' errors as a result of centuries of textual transmission.

> Here I follow Tov (1992:315) who says that biblical books passed through two main stages of development: the stage of the book's literary growth, and the stage of the copying and textual transmission of the completed compositions. . . literary criticism deals with the first area, the stage of the development of the biblical books, whereas textual criticism operates within the second stage, that of the book's copying and transmission.

> Between *preferred reading* and *correct reading,* I favour the former.

2   On the other hand a text external approach seeks to understand the Old Testament from without; that is to say in the light of archaeology, near eastern setting and near eastern studies.

3   The Old Testament writers also made use of written sources (eg *Book of the Wars of Yahweh* in Num 21:14, Exod 17:14; *Book of the Upright* in Josh 10:13–14; 2 Sam 1:17; *Book of the Lord* in Isa 34:16, Book of Kings used either used by the Chronicler or both using common sources, etc.).

4   See Asrid Beck and James A Sanders, 'The Leningrad Codex: Rediscovering the Oldest Complete Bible', in *Bible Review* (1997:32–41;46). Aaron Ben Asher who vocalised and accented the text was recognised as the undisputed Masorete who had the final word.

5   Aron Dotan from Tel Aviv University is working on a critical edition of The Pentateuch Codex Or. 4445 which he claimed preceded Ben Asher and the name of the masoretic scribe is Nissi ben Daniel Ha-Cohen. Its value lies in its pre- Ben Asher traits and as an authentic representative of another independent masoretic school (in a communique given at the *Society for Biblical Literature* Meeting at Budapest 1995).

6   This high figure given by Schiffman has been disputed by Geza Vermes in his book review of 'Reclaiming the Dead Sea Scrolls', *Biblical Archaeology Review* 21/2 (1995):6–10. Following Tov's revision, Schiffman puts the proto-masoretic texts as 40%. This is also the view of Eugene Ulrich in a personal conversation with the me at the 1995 *Society for Biblical Literature* Meeting in Budapest. The reply of Schiffman to Geza Vermes in *Biblical Archaeology Review* 21/4 (1995):20 is,

> The revised figures of Emanuel Tov do not change the fact that the proto-Masoretic type is the largest and that, taken together with those types ultimately derived from it, it constitutes the majority of the Qumran Biblical manuscripts. Accordingly, I stand by my statement that the Qumran manu-

scripts prove that the proto-Masoretic text type was dominant in Hasmonean Palestine.

7   I summarise the main ideas from Ulrich's work concerning the composition of Books of Scripture as seen from the Qumran:
     Composition of Scriptures was organic, developmental, with successive layers of tradition. Although traditional material was faithfully retold and handed down from generation to generation, it was also creatively expanded and reshaped to fit the new circumstances and new needs experienced through the vicissitudes of history.
     By so doing they were adding to it, enriching it making it relevant by up dating. The texts were authoritative and through the traditional process they were being made more authoritative. Thus they became part of the 'canonical process'. The works of the scribes may be described as repetition and resignification.
     See Eugene Ulrich, 'The Bible in the Making: The Scriptures at Qumran,' in Eugene Ulrich and James Vanderkam (eds), *The Community of the Renewed Covenant* (Notre Dame, Indiana: University of Notre Dame Press,1994):77–93.

8   For a recent study on the canon, see Roger Beckwith, *The Old Testament Canon of the Old Testament Church* (Grand Rapids: William B. Eerdmans, 1985); Lee Martin McDonald, *The Formation of the Christian Biblical Canon* (Peabody, Massachusetts: Hendrickson Publishers, 1995 [rev ed of 1988]) and John Barton, *Holy Writings, Sacred Text: The Canon of Early Christianity* (Louisville, Kentucky: Westminster John Knox, 1997) and Stephen Dempster, 'An "Extraordinary Fact": Torah and Temple and the Contours of the Hebrew Canon', Part 1 and 2 in *Tyndale Bulletin* 48:1 (1997):23–66; 48:2 (1997):191–218 and Moshe Halbertal, *People of the Book : Canon, Meaning and Authority* (Harvard University Press, 1997).
     See also Goldingay (1994:138–167) on the development of the Jewish and Christian Canon; Schnabel (1995:16–24) Barrera (1997) and Davies (1998).

9   How the Masoretic text type eventually supplanted all others is not entirely clear. Neither do we have evidence of an official promulgation by the rabbinate.

10   A uniform textual tradition becomes necessary when there is no longer appeal to divine inspiration and when the authority outside Scripture shifted to Scripture itself.

11   For more details, see Adam S. van der Woude, 'Pluriformity and Uniformity: Reflections on the Transmission of the Text of the Old Testament', J. N. Bremmer and F. Garcia Martinez (eds) in *Sacred History and Sacred Texts in Early Judaism: A Symposium in Honour of A. S. van der Woude* (Kampen, Netherlands: Kok Pharos, 1992):151–170. For a comprehensive survey see, Mulder (1988: 39–136).

12   For scribal reliability in the accurate rendition of the traditional text and accurate transmission of historical data see David W. Baker, 'Scribes as Transmitters of Traditions', in A. R. Millard, J. K. Hoffmeier and David W. Baker, *Faith, Tradition, and History: Old Testament Historiography in Its Near Eastern Context*

(Winona Lake, Indiana: Eisenbrauns, 1994): 65–78; Alan R. Millard, 'In Praise of Ancient Scribes', *Biblical Archaeologist* 45 (1982:143–153); Wurthein (1979:12–27); For a discussion on the role of the scribes and the masoretes in the Transmission of the Text, see Mulder (1988:87–136); Eugene Ulrich, 'The Canonical Process, Textual Criticism, and later stages in the Composition of the Bible', in Michael Fishbane and Emanuel Tov (eds), Shaarei Talmon: *Studies in the Bible, Qumran and the Ancient Near East Presented to Shemaryahu Talmon* (Winona Lake, Indiana: Eisenbrauns, 1992):267–295.

13   A case in point is the Balaam Text of the MT where the vowel pointings *appear* to make little or no sense at all. This does help to bolster the points raised by Barr.

14   See, Shlemo Morag, 'On the Historical Validity of the Vocalization of the Hebrew Bible', *Journal of the American Oriental Society* 94 (1974):307–315; For a more detailed discussion, see Tov (1992:39–48), Goshen-Gottstein, 'The Aleppo Codex and the Rise of the Masoretic Bible', *Biblical Archaeologist* 42/1979:145–163 and also 'The Rise of the Tiberian Bible Text', in Alexander Altman (ed) *Studies and Texts* 1963:79–122; D. S. Loewinger, 'The Aleppo Codex and the Ben Asher Tradition', *Textus 1* (1960):59–74. James Barr, *Comparative Philology and the Text of the Old Testament* (London: SCM,1968): 188–222 in chapter 7 on 'The Massoretes, Vocalization and Emendation.'

It needs to be pointed out that the Masoretic text is not identical with the canonical text, but is only a vehicle for its recovery. There is no extant canonical text. Rather, what we have is a Hebrew text which has been carefully transmitted and meticulously guarded by a school of scribes through an elaborate Masoretic system.

As Childs (1979:100) adds,

. . . even though the expressed purpose of the Masoretes was to preserve the canonical text unchanged, in fact, a variety of factors make clear that changes have occurred and that a distinction between the MT and the canonical text must be maintained.

At the same time I do not underestimate the value of the Greek Septuagint since it is an important textual witness to the Old Testament (1000 years earlier than the MT) and the fact that the New Testament writers used it in their quotations. The discovery of the Dead Sea Scrolls has helped to heighten its importance.

Chapter Seven

An Attitude of Reading

'Would you tell me, please, which way I ought to go from here?' 'That depends a good deal on where you want to get to,' said the cat 'I don't much care where—' said Alice 'Then it doesn't matter which way you go,' said the cat.

(Carroll 1962:87)

7.1 Priorities

7.1.1 Synchronic rather than Diachronic[1]

In any exegetical enterprise of the text, priority should be given to the synchronic reading (focuses on the meaning of the text as it now stands regardless of its prehistory) rather than a diachronic (concerns with the historical development/background of the biblical text and how a text arrived at its present form). Any attempt to go behind the text to discover oral traditions, sources or process of formation of the final text though valuable in itself does not help much in understanding the meaning.

As Barr (1983b:169) explains

> . . . historical study has too often acted as if the diachronic study of change is the first and only step. Against this it could well be urged that the synchronic study of the documents and the social states logically precedes, rather than follows, the diachronic study of change.

7.1.2 Text rather than Event

A distinction needs to be made between an event (an occurrence or something that happens in time and space) and a text which refers to something that is written and comprises words, sentences, paragraph, etc. (Sailhamer 1992:8–22). Events are things that happened in the past and can be reconstructed whereas texts are composed of language that follows certain conventions.

It is to be acknowledged that understanding the background and culture may throw some light on the text but may not explain the text. Its validity is not denied but its suitability for exegesis is debatable. One common assumption in exegesis is that the more we know about the background information of Israel culturally, historically, geographically, etc., (its Near Eastern setting), the more we can understand the book. To a certain extent this is true. Archaeology and history of religion are useful in themselves but must not be confused with exegesis which is to explain the text.

According to Schökel (1974:13),

> The reader and interpreter of a text have only the text before themselves, not a preexistent or underlying meaning. It is the task of the reader and interpreter to perceive and explain all the significant marks of the text as well as its configuration.

However, if an exegete is not careful he may be led astray due to a distortion of semantic information. Understanding a subject matter does not equal understanding the message or even the meaning of the text. This kind of approach is more suitable for doing a history of religion rather than exegesis. A text immanent approach affirms the sufficiency of the text and that text can be understood within and not without.

The focus of exegesis should not be on what happened (event) but what is recorded (text). The reason is that 'when events are exegeted, multiple perspectives arise' but 'when texts are exegeted we can receive a privileged perspective of the writer of the text' (Sailhamer 1986:291).

7.1.3 Source Language rather than its Cognate

An important question that needs to be asked is where does one look for the meaning of a word when the writer does not explain? Barr's (1961, 1968, 1992) contribution in this field is invaluable. I shall sketch and summarise his views.

His suggestion is that we begin with the source language. When the source language meaning differs from a cognate language, priority of meaning must be accorded to the source language. In other words, instead of going outside the confines of the canon, for a general understanding of the term and then fitting into the text, it is better to go back to the text and see how it is related to another text in a broader unit within the canon. For example, to explicate a Hebrew word, we should seek its meaning within the Hebrew language (classical and post biblical Hebrew first rather than using other semitic languages to elucidate the term).

Through time, a word might have undergone semantic changes and might be used in a different sense in Hebrew. Hence there is a need to exercise caution in assuming that lexical elements found in one Semitic language will be shared by another. Granted there may be certain stock parallelism held in common with pre-Israelite poetry.[2] Even items may be formally identical with Canaanite or Ugaritic materials. His dictum is 'a word has meaning only within its own language and its own period of usage' (Barr 1992:141).

In sum, comparative philology should only be used as the last resort when encountering *hapax legomena*.

Some other important principles laid down by Barr (1968) are:

1) Word study must be linguistic rather than logical in character.
2) A distinction should be made between referents and information.
3) Meaning should be established in one language only. We must not define the meaning of a word in Hebrew by thinking what it means in another language. Meaning in Hebrew is independent of meaning in Arabic and depends on the choices within the Hebrew Lexical stock of a given time.
4) The use of philological treatment from other cognate languages are approximate and probabilistic rather than exact and decisive since our knowledge of semantic development is hypothetical and indirect.
5) Precise references, nuances, and overtone should not be decided on evidence of cognates but by the Hebrew context itself.
6) One value of the comparative approach is that it has set free senses, which are likely in the Hebrew context, from domination by derivations reached from within Hebrew alone.
7) Chronological and geographical proximities are important. That is to say sources nearer to OT in time might be considered more likely to produce solutions as well as sources nearer to Palestine might be more reliable. Even if it is late, it might go back to similar or earlier cultural conditions and might retain traces of common vocabulary. Hebrew has closer affinity with the classification of North west semitic family rather than south—eg Ethiopic, and East Akkadian.

7.2 Performance[3]

7.2.1 Read it Responsibly

Hermeneutical protocol suggests that we read a text responsibly. Responsible reading requires us to seek first the nature of the text's communicative intent (genre, sense) before seeking to evaluate or use the text (Vanhoozer). That is to say we must receive the text on its own term. And when we have understood the sense of the text (ie allow it to fulfil its communicative aim), we can then evaluate its significance or critique it.

To put it in another way, submission before question, understanding before criticism and interpretation before use (Vanhoozer). Part of this responsible reading is to receive the text on its own terms and 'let go and let the text have its way.' As Steiner (1979) remarks, 'a reader has two roles: as a critic he functions at a distance from the text like a judge and a master; but as a reader he *serves* the text and is like a shepherd.'[4] The difference between reading and using a text is that the former reads it in order to discover something about its nature but the latter starts from it in order to get something (Eco 1990:57).[5] Vanhoozer's (1993:377) point is poignant when he says that when we 'disregard the rights of the text' and insist that the text has no determinate meaning it leads to an interpretative rape.'

7.2.2 Read it Receptively

In reading, readers should not begin with the premise that all texts are suspects. Is it not a fundamental axiom that a text is innocent until proven guilty? Should we not practise a "hermeneutics of trust" (or the "hermeneutics of consent" to use Stuhlmacher's phrase)[6] by suspending judgement of mistrust and disbelief that say, 'this isn't real; it's just a story' (Schneiders 1991:173)?[7] Eventually, a "hermeneutics of suspicion" will lead to 'poisoning the well from which water may be drawn' (Vanhoozer).

Hayes (1997:291;222) correctly argues that a hermeneutics of trust does not mean 'accepting everything in the text at face value', but rather it is 'necessarily a matter of [being] faithful to hear and discern'. Maier (1994:57) also affirms that the 'starting point of exegesis is not scientific scepticism because it is rooted in Cartesian thinking which says all that lies outside the thinking self is to be doubted but rather obeyed.'

As Steiner (1992:312) argues:

> We venture a leap : we grant ab initio that there is 'something there' to be understood, that the transfer will not be void. All understanding and the demonstrative statement of understanding which is where translation starts with an act of trust.

Reader receptivity means we keep our eyes and fingers on the text (Kaiser) by paying close attention to the sign posts along the way. Privileging the world of the text exposes the reader to the textual world which in turn can enlarge self understanding. It also means becoming alert for strategic clues given by the writer.

Perhaps the irony of the 'hermeneutics of trust' is that unknowingly it will challenge us to 'be suspicious—suspicious first of ourselves, because our minds have been corrupted and shaped by the present evil age' (Hayes 1997:221). This will lead to mental renewal and spiritual transformation.

A receptive reading of the text enables the reader to ultimately 'experience the power and the pleasures of the text' (Scholes 1985:41).

Gomes (1996:34-35) sums it best when he says,

> The element of trust enters into the art of interpretation of scripture when we understand that the Bible comes to us as a trust both from God and from the people of God. It is the record of holy encounters between people and God, encounters that have been reckoned to be decisive and compelling, and that have been preserved from generation to generation because they remind each generation of the presence of God in their lives and the search for God when the divine absence is felt. . .We trust the text . . . because in its infinite variety it points to the truth and communicates truth because it comes from the truth which we call God.

7.2.3 Read it Respectfully[8]

The text is composed or compiled by somebody at some time in the past for some purpose in some places.[9] It did not come out accidentally or out of an explosion. We should treat the work of that writer(s) respectfully as we treat a human being. For Ferguson (1986:83), respectful reading of the text means

> . . . that the interpreter must be subservient to the text itself—that is the interpreter must allow the text to determine its interpretation. In order to understand the text, the interpreter must 'stand under', listen to, hear the text and not impose a foreign meaning into it.

To treat a text respectfully, is to ' entertain its perspective and to heed its voice' (Vanhoozer). By so doing 'the text thus restored to life, is able to give something back in turn' (Vanhoozer 1993:382). A respectful reading requires some amount of humility because

> we do not know all that we need to know. We do not know all that 'they knew. We do know, however, that what we have is what they have left to us, and that translating that treasure from their time into ours and back again is an enterprise that calls for patience, endurance, diligence, skill, and perhaps above all, humility. Arrogance in reading these texts is perhaps an even greater sin than unbelief. . .
>
> (Gomes 1996:51–52)[10]

7.2.4 Read it Regularly

To comprehend a text, we need to read as often as we can because communication is a complex process. The more attention one gives to the text, the greater our understanding will be. The same goes for listening and obeying the text.

7.2.5 Read it Reflectively

The Bible is a book that requires deep reflection because of the content. A hurried reading will not yield rich dividends. The metaphor (imperfect as it may be) that comes to my mind concerning reflective reading is tantamount to a tourist travelling to a foreign country for sightseeing and cultural immersion. To capture some of the scenic beauty, he uses cameras and cam recorders. In between journeys he takes breaks for refreshments. To get the most out of a trip, he will need to ask questions and also enlist the help of a tourist guide.[11] At home if he wants to relive some of those memorable experiences, he looks at the photographs or watches videos and makes plans to go back again to visit.

7.2.6 Read it Raptly

Give attention to it. As we listen attentively, we can then respond appropriately. Listening comes before speaking and not the other way round. Any time we reverse the process we show disrespect and our responses will be wrong because we are breaking the most fundamental rule in communications: Before we speak we must first listen. On the other hand, just because we have heard the message does not mean we have understood it. Therefore, it is prudent to be attentive. By failing to give rapt attention to the text, 'the reader becomes Lord of his own hermeneutical ring' (Vanhoozer).

7.2.7 Read it Resourcefully

This can be done by using various tools such as lexica, concordance, commentaries, study guides, dictionaries, etc. These are some of the important tools to aid us in our understanding of the text. Their value lies in the fact that they have been written by capable scholars many of whom are specialists who spend a greater part of their lives producing them. We can certainly expect depth as well as breadth in their specialisation.

7.2.8 Read it Religiously

Biblical texts are theologically oriented. Hence a proper reading of the texts must be oriented towards understanding the *Majesty* since the Bible is the Word of God for humanity. Hence even though faith is not a prerequisite for interpreting the biblical texts, it is a precondition for truly understanding them.

As Schneiders (1991:178) articulates,

> The text is a privileged mediator of encounter between God and humanity. For believers it is the *revelatory text* and must be pursued with relentless love by

those who believe that the text is a privileged mediator of encounter between God and humanity.

7.3 Hermeneutical Responsibilities

Whatever strategies we employ in reading a text we should 'obey the law of the text'. According to Jeanrond (1982:11), the law of the text 'consists of instructions to be followed by the reader and of open spaces to be filled by the reader.' This law is liberating rather than inhibiting. Since every textual content has a textual form, 'interpretation is responsible when we follow the arrows of the textual sense' (ibid:6). Understanding develops when a reader obeys the primary communicative perspective of the text and follows its movement from what it says to what it talks about.

The communicative perspective of biblical texts is aimed at 'unfolding the primary communicative perspective that Jesus is Christ [NT] and Yahweh is God [OT]' (Jeanrond 1982:11). In other words, the written word points to the Living Word.

McEvenue (1994:49) underscores a very important point when he contends that

> a reader will understand a text in so far as he correctly identifies the thing (subject matter, object, etc.) about which the text speaks, and successfully negotiates a reciprocal illumination of the thing by the text, and of the text by the thing.

The goal of interpretation should be an appropriation that leads to action. Appropriation[12] does not consist of 'making the text one's own nor extracting information but of surrendering oneself to the text' (Vanhoozer). Surrendering oneself to the text is one certain way of entering into and living in the world of the text. Moreover, interpretation appropriates the text only what the text communicates. There is a need to safeguard misappropriation of the text. One possible safeguard against total arbitrariness of appropriation of the text is to call upon 'the community of readers' (Jeanrond 1982:12–13). In the final analysis, as a reader,

> I still stand before the law of the ethics of reading, subject to it, compelled by it, persuaded of its existence and sovereignty by what happens to me when I read. What happens is the experience of an 'I must. . .'
>
> (Millar 1987:127)

Notes

1   For a brief but sane discussion on the interplay between synchronic and diachronic, confer with Lim (1997):19–21.

  See also Vern Poythress, 'Analysing A Biblical Text: Some Important Linguistic Distinction', *Scottish Journal of Theology* 32 (1979):113–137 and 'Analysing Biblical Text: What Are We After?', *Scottish Journal of Theology* 32 (1979):319–331.

2   A fault readily committed by philologists because of their (over?) eagerness to find parallelism between the semitic languages. See Lim (1997):90–105 on the pitfalls and potentials of parallelism.

3   'Interpreting the Bible is like a musician's performance of a score. The notes delimit what a musician may play. At the same time, an entertaining performance depends on the musician's artistic virtuosity within that delimitation' (Lim 1997: footnote 199).

4   See George Steiner, 'Critic/Reader', *New Literary History* 10 (1979):423–452.

5   Cf Kirsten (1995) who says that responsible interpretation requires the reader towards finding a possible 'first meaning' of the text but also to the *Wirkungsgeschichte* of the biblical text. Responsible interpretation presupposes that we acknowledge the power used in connection with the interpretation of texts and the misuse of power that may take place in the name of the text. All interpretations must be regarded as a basis for discussion and the responsibilities of the exegete may be termed as openness, respect, expectations, willingness to listen, willingness to criticize and willingness to be agents of change. Finally, the metaphor of friendship is a good beginning for creating an ethics of interpretation (partners in dialogue may be another apt metaphor). This paper was read at the Society for Biblical Literature (1995) at Budapest.

6   See Peter Stulmacher, *Historical Criticism and Theological Interpretation of Scripture: Toward a Hermeneutic of Consent* (Philadelphia: Fortress, 1977).

7   See Hans Weder, 'Kritik am Verdacht', *Zeitschrift für die Theologie und Kirche* 91:3 (1996):59–83.

8   Cf. Seitz (1998:11) who says there is a need for 'the cultivation of a proper respect—reverence is not too strong a term—for what an honor it is to read this literature [Old Testament] at all.'

9   Cf 'Our task as exegetes is not to adapt the text in order to conform it to our ideas of what a book should look like but to read the text carefully in order to search for its own structure and meaning' (Smelik 1996:282–283) in Klaas A. D. Smelik, 'Letters to the Exiles: Jeremiah 29 in Context', *Scandinavian Journal of the Old Testament* 10:2 (1996):282–295.

10   Consider the plea of Rendtorff (1998:44):

   Here I would only plead for a new humility towards the text of the Bible. We have to interpret it, not change it. The Bible, in its final, canonical form, is always our teacher.

11   Curiously, not much has been written on the role of the Holy Spirit [tourist guide] in relation to hermeneutics. For an orientation to the work of the Holy Spirit in general, see Clark H. Pinock, *Flame of Love: A Theology of the Holy Spirit* (Illinois, Downers Grove: Intervarsity Press, 1998); Wilf Hidebrabdt, *An Old Testament Theology of the Spirit of God* (Peabody: Hendrickson, 1995) and a series of articles on the Holy Spirit in *Ex Auditu* 12 (1996).

12   There are three dimensions to a text—understanding, explication and application (Gadamer) while Jeanrond puts it as understanding, validation and appropriation (Jeanrond).
   For the use of practical application, see Jeffrey Arnold, *Discovering the Bible for Yourself* (Downers Grove, Illinois: Intervarsity Press, 1993); G. Waldemar Degner, 'From Text to Context: Hermeneutical Principles for Applying the Word of God,' *Concordia Theological Quarterly* 60:4 (1996):259–278; Brian A. Shealy, 'Redrawing the Line Between Hermeneutics and Application', *Master's Seminary Journal* 8:1 (1997):83–105; A. Berkeley and Alvera M. Mickelsen, *Understanding Scripture: How to Read and Study the Bible* (Peabody, Massachusetts: Hendrikson Publishers, 1992).

Chapter Eight

By Way of Conclusion

It is one thing to study well water, to smell it, to analyze its chemical composition, and quite another thing to drink. One who continually suspects well water of contamination and never drinks will never quench his or her thirst. The reader at the well, in order to be nourished, must draw from and drink of the text. To "drink" here means to accept and appropriate. The reader has a responsibility to receive the text according to its nature and intention. . . One can do many things with water from a well; but in the desert of criticism, a drink should be received with eagerness and thanks.

(Vanhoozer 1995a:325)

8.1 Hermeneutical Observations

1) Scripture can be called text because we presuppose the arrangement of the marks in certain shapes written in black ink on the pages to have a role to play.

2) Texts express themselves through the signs of language that have phonological, lexical and syntactic structures which are time conditioned.

3) Language functions on the basis of preestablished conventions and is by nature a structured system. The use of words limit each other in a reciprocal manner from their literary context which constitute particularity of meaning communicated by a given text (eg when we say inside we mean something different from outside).

4) Every reader is an interpreter who brings with him certain assumptions, presuppositions, etc. when reading a text which in turn influences his interpretation. A text cannot be divorced from the context of the interpreter.

5) Distanciation must antecede fusion of horizons in order to clarify hermeneutical options.

6) Accurate interpretation depends on accurate reading of the Text which in turn depends on asking the right questions.

7) Right application depends on right interpretation. What the text meant should precede what the text means. Exegesis must precede eisegesis.

8) The intended message of the Text is distorted when we refuse to read it according to its own term of reference (eg literary genre, literary context, etc.). To appropriate the text, we must listen to come to the Text.

9) Human words written long ago can be understood as God's word because of the Incarnation. Therefore the Bible is to be approached both as human script and divine scripture that has past, present and future relevance.

10) Scripture must be interpreted like any book yet not like any other book because of the 'Majesty of the Subject'.[1]

11) Spoken words can communicate effectively the written word when we encounter the Living Word.

12) Biblical texts are essentially theological texts.

8.2 Postscript

To say that each interpreter brings a particular hermeneutical theory to the text the interpreter is reading, is no longer challenged today. Consciously or unconsciously, all interpreters bring their presuppositions and assumptions to bear in the acts of interpretation. Our reading of texts is filtered through our own philosophical assumptions and theological inclinations.

As responsible interpreters of the Word, we are required to identify and to be aware of our own presuppositions, to pay attention to previous scholarship and be vigilant in interacting with the text. Such acts may help to contain if not suppress any idiosyncratic interpretations.

However sophisticated the interpretive methodologies are, if they do not help us understand the texts, they need to be consigned to the museum of obscurity. After all, the goal of hermeneutics is understanding the texts. For that reason I would argue that the validity of any method(s) of interpretation is dependent on accomplishing what it was designed to do. Reading strategies which do justice to the text consist of text internal rather than text external, synchronic rather than diachronic, hermeneutic of trust rather than hermeneutic of suspicion, reader receptivity rather than reader response and reading out rather than reading in.

Sartre makes an excellent point when he says 'You are perfectly free, to leave the book on the table. But if you open it, you assume responsibility for it'.[2] He is right. The moment we open any book we must assume responsibility because texts have rights.[3] This means resisting the impulse to force the text to mean what we want it to say but rather to 'let go and the text have its way.' In other words, 'we are free agents; we have to come to terms with the restraints the text imposes' (Quinn 1992:18). This is our hermeneutical responsibility as readers of the texts.

If we refuse, we hold the texts hostage and put the texts at the mercy of interpreters. The consequence will be that we can prove almost anything from the text. Since there is no way we can judge a false reading, different forms of propagandistic and deviant social norms can be justified. In other words, anytime we *massage* a text to mean what we want it to mean, we are guilty of committing textual *harassment*, textual *strangulation* as well as textual *manipulation*.

Readers may ask, why is there so much fuss about the text? Why should we pay so much attention to the text? What is so special about the text? Scholes' (1985:165) response is very penetrative.

> Who cares about the text? We all do. We care about texts for many reasons, not the least of which is that they bring us news that alters our way of interpreting things. If this were not the case, the Gospels and the teachings of Karl Marx would have fallen upon deaf ears. Textual power is ultimately power to change the world.

When the textual claim of the Biblical texts is acknowledged, the effect of reading can be provocative and transformative when we are 'open to transcendence' (Stuhlmacher).[4] To be open to transcendence is to open ourselves 'to the word of God, which speaks through the text' and 'to the changes of the horizon of interpretation through the word of God' (Jeanrond 1988:53). Put it in another way, scripture emits 'Signals of Transcendence' (Berger) to those who are willing to listen sympathetically to the text's witness concerning God and human experience. Inevitably, the horizon of both the reader and the text will be fused resulting in modification, consolidation or negation.

The reader needs to be caught up in the text or get lost in it in order for the text to function as a 'transformative mediation of meaning' (Schneiders). Transformative interpretation is a 'conscious effort toward life integration through self transcendence toward the horizon of ultimate value '(Schneiders 1991:174). Newton (1995:292) adds that 'texts tax readers with ethical duties which increase in proportion to the measure with which they are taken up. The ethics of reading is to think the infinite, the transcendent, the Stranger.'

Scripture is a place of our encounter with God. However, 'it is an encounter in the dark which, if one wrestle with all our might and hang on until the light dawns, may yet earn for us a blessing even as it leaves us longing in our journey into the future of faith' (Schneiders 1993:35).

Hayes (1997:22) drives home the point concerning goal of interpretation when he argues,

> The real work of interpretation is to hear the text. We must consider how to read and teach scripture in a way that opens up its message and both models and fosters trust in God. So much of the ideological critique that currently dominates the academy fails to foster these qualities. Scripture is critiqued but never interpreted. The critic exposes but never exposits. Thus the word recedes into the background and we are left talking only about the politics of interpretation, having lost the capacity to perform interpretations.[5]

Perhaps, a modern tragedy of reading biblical texts is that on one hand we are trying 'to devise a way of reading the Word of God, from which no word of God ever comes'(Langmead).[6] On the other hand, an (over) confidence in techniques and methodologies will lead us to 'deceive ourselves into thinking that our words are God's word' (Fowl and Jones 1991:110).

Conceivably, what prevents us from hearing the Word of God is our *theological tone deafness* (Childs' term). At the same time, what persuades us to resist the Word of God is our *scholastic chutzpa*. Could the solution for the former be a new hearing aid and the latter a heart transplant?

Notes

1   At the same time I am mindful of the fable of the six blind Hindustani who are asked to describe an elephant. Each one of them gives a different interpretation of what an elephant is based on the part that person touches. One moral of the fable is that too often we mistake the parts for the whole. However, very often, the most important part of the equation has been left out ie, the king who brought the elephant into the room knows what the animal looks like and sees everything from his vantage position. He is the one telling the story.

2   Quoted by Newton (1995:19).

3   On the other hand, Patte (1995) in his book, *Ethics of Biblical Interpretation* (Louisville, Kentucky: Westminster John Knox), goes so far as to see ethical responsibility as acknowledging the legitimacy of several critical readings of a given text. In line with postmodernism, he is ambivalent on several points. Although he raises a few issues, but is short on providing answers. His focus is more in andro critical exegesis. For a summary of his theses, see pages 113–132.

4   Exegesis is truly faithful to proper intention of biblical texts when it goes not only to the heart of the formulation to find the reality of faith there expressed but also seeks to link this reality to the experience of faith in our present world (A document from the Pontifical Biblical commission in Houlden 1995:49–50). 'Access to a proper understanding of biblical texts is only granted to the person who has an affinity with what the text is saying on the basis of life experience' (ibid).

5   In other words, 'If our critical readings lead us away from trusting the grace of God in Jesus Christ, then something is amiss, and we would do well to interrogate the methods and presuppositions that have taught us to distance ourselves arrogantly or fearfully from the text and to miss scripture's gracious word of promise' (Hayes 1997:222).

6   Quoted by Stott (1992:216).

Bibliography

Aageson, James W.
   1993   *Written Also for Our Sake: Paul and the Art of Biblical Interpretation* (Westminster: John Knox)

Adam, A. K. M.
   1995   *What is Postmodern Biblical Criticism?* (Minneapolis: Fortress Press)

Addinall, Peter
   1991   *Philosophy and Biblical Interpretation* (Cambridge: Cambridge University Press)

Armstrong, Paul B.
   1990   *Conflicting Readings: Variety and Validity in Interpretation* (Chapel Hill: The University of North Carolina)
   1983   'The Conflict of Interpretation and the Limits of Pluralism', *Publication of the Modern Language Association of America* 98:341–352

Atkins, G. Douglas and Laura Morrow (ed.)
   1989   *Contemporary Literary Theory* (New York: Macmillan)

Baldick, Chris
   1990   *The Concise Oxford Dictionary of Literary Terms* (Oxford: Oxford University Press)

Barr, James
   1961   *The Semantics of Biblical Language* (London: Oxford University Press)
   1962   *Biblical Words for Time* (London: Oxford University Press)

1968   *Comparative Philology and the Text of the Old Testament* (London:SCM)

1973a   *The Bible in the Modern World* (London: SCM Press, reissued 1990)

1973b   'Reading the Bible as Literature', *Bulletin of the John Rylands Library* 56/1:10–33

1983b   *Holy Scripture: Canon, Authority, Criticism* (Philadelphia: Westminster)

1992   'Hebrew Lexicography', in Walter R. Bodine (ed), *Linguistics and Biblical Hebrew* (Winona Lake: Eisenbrauns): 137–151

1993a   *Biblical Faith and Natural Theology* (Oxford: Clarendon Press)

1993b   'Scope and Problems in the Semantics of Classical Hebrew', *Zeitschrift für Althebraistik* 6/1 1993:3–14

Barrera, Julio Trebolle

1998   *The Jewish and Christian Bible: An Introduction to the History of the Bible* (trans. Wilfred G.E. Watson; Grand Rapids: Eerdmans)

Barthes, Roland

1968   'Death of the Author', *The Rustle of Language* (New York: Hill and Wang): 53–55

1977   *Image—Music—Text* (Glasgow: Fontana)

Barton, John

1984   'Classifying Biblical Criticism', *Journal for the Study of the Old Testament* 29:19–35

1987   'Reading the Bible as Literature: Two Questions for Biblical Critics', *Journal of Literature and Theology* 1/2:135–153

1993   *The Future of Old Testament Study* (Oxford: Clarendon Press)

1994   'Historical Criticism and Literary Interpretation: Is There any Common Ground?' in Stanley E. Porter, Paul Joyce and David Orton (eds), *Crossing the Boundaries: Essays in Biblical Interpretation in Honour of Michael D. Goulder* (Leiden: E. J. Brill)

1997   *Holy Writings, Sacred texts: The Canon in Early Christianity* (Philadelphia: Westminster/John Knox Press)

Bauman, Zygmunt
    1992   *Hermeneutics and Social Science* (England: Gregg Revivals)

Beardsley, Moore
    1970   *The Possibility of Criticism* (Detroit: Wayne State University Press)

Belsey, Catherine
    1980   *Critical Practice* (London: Routledge, rep. 1994)

Berlin, Adele
    1983   *Poetics and Interpretation of Biblical Narrative* (Sheffield: Almond)
    1991   'Hermeneutics,' in Jason P. Rosenblatt and Joseph C. Sitterson, Jr. (eds), *Not in Heaven: Coherence and Complexity in Biblical Narrative* (Bloomington and Indianapolis:Indiana University Press)

Best, Steven and Douglas Kellner
    1991   *Postmodernism Theory: Critical Investigation* (New York: The Guilford Press)

Bonycastle, Stephen
    1991   *In Search of Authority: An Introductory Guide to Literary Theory* (Canada: Broadview)

Bordo, Susan
    1987   *The Flight to Objectivity : Essays on Cartesianism and Culture* (Albany: State University of New York Press)

Brown, Delwin
    1994   *Boundaries of our Habitation: Tradition and Theological Construction* (State University of New York: State University of New York Press)

Bruns, Gerald L.
    1984   'Canon and the Power in the Hebrew Scriptures', *Critical Inquiry* 10:462–480

Brueggemann, Walter
    1997   *Theology of the Old Testament: Testimony, Dispute, Advocacy* (Minneapolis: Fortress Press)

Burke, Sean
    1992   *The Death and Return of the Author* (Edinburgh:
           Edinburgh University Press)

Callaway, Mary C.
    1993   'Canonical Criticism', in Stephen L. Mackenzie and Stephen
           R. Haynes (eds), in *To Each His Own Meaning* (London:
           Geoffrey Chapman)

Castelli, Elizabeth E. and Stephen D. Moore (eds)
    1995   *The Postmodern Bible* (New Haven: Yale University Press)

Childs, Brevard
    1978   'The Exegetical Significance of Canon for the Study of the
           Old Testament', in *Vetus Testamentum* Supplements 29
           (Göttingen Congress Volume; Leiden: E.J.Brill):66–80
    1979   *Introduction to the Old Testament as Scripture* (Phila-
           delphia: Fortress)
    1983   *The New Testament as Canon* (Philadelphia: Fortress
           Press)
    1985   *Old Testament Theology in Canonical Context* (Phila-
           delphia: Fortress Press)
    1992   *Biblical Theology of the Old and New Testaments* (Lon-
           don: SCM Press Ltd)

Corti, Maria
    1978   *An Introduction to Literary Semiotics* (trans. Margherita
           Bogat and Allen Mandelbaum: Bloomington : Indiana Uni-
           versity Press)

Crystal, David
    1992   *An Encyclopedia Dictionary of Language and Languages*
           (England: Penguin Books)

Cuddon, J. A.
    1992   *The Penguin Dictionary of Literary Terms and Literary
           Theory* (London: Penguinn Books, 3rd edn)

Culler, Jonathan
    1981   *The Pursuit of Signs: Semiotics; Literature,
           Deconstructionism* (Ithaca: Cornell University Press)
    1982   *On Deconstructionism: Theory and Criticism after Struc-
           turalism* (Ithaca: Cornell University Press)

Davies, Philip R.
  1998   *Scribes and Schools: The Canonization of the Hebrew Scriptures* (Philadelphia: Westminster/John Knox)

de Beaugrande, Rober-Alain and Wolfgang Ulrich Dressler
  1981   *Introduction to Text Linguistics* (London: Longman)

Detweiler, Robert
  1985   'What is a Sacred Text?', in Reader Response Approaches to Biblical and Secular Texts, *Semeia* 31:213–230

Dickens, Charles
  1859   *A Tale of Two Cities* (London: Penguin Books [rep 1994])

Dockery, David S.
  1992   *Biblical Interpretation: Then and Now* (Grand Rapids, Michigan: Baker)

Dockery, David S.
  1995   'The Challenge of Postmodernism,' in David S. Dockery (ed), *The Challenge of Postmodernism: An Evangelical Engagement* (Wheaton, Illinois, 1995):13–18

Dunn, James D. G.
  1995   'Historical Text as Historical Text: Some Basic Hermeneutical Reflections in Relation to the New Testament'in Jon Davies, Graham Harvey and Wilfred G. E. Watson (eds),*Words Remembered, Texts Renewed: Essays in Honour of John F. A. Sawyer* (JSOTSup 195; Sheffield:Sheffield Academic Press):340–359

Eagleton, Terry
  1983   *Literary Theory: An Introduction* (Oxford: Blackwell)
  1990   *The Significance of Theory* (Oxford: Oxford University Press)

Eco, Umberto
  1979   *A Theory of Semiotics* (Bloomington: Indiana University Press)
  1990   *The Limits of Interpretation* (Bloomington: Indiana University Press)
  1993   *Interpretation and Overinterpretation* (Cambridge: Cambridge University Press)

Edgerton, W. Dow
    1992   *The Passion of Interpretation* (Louisville, Kentucky: John Knox Press)

Ernesti, J.A
    1824   Elements of Interpretation (trans. Moses Stuart; Andover: Flagg and Gould)

Fee, Gordon and Douglas Stuart
    1981   *How to Read the Bible for All Its Worth* (Grand Rapids, Michigan: Zondervan)

Ferguson, Duncan S.
    1986   *Biblical Hermeneutics: An Introduction* (London: SCM Press)

Fishbane, Michael
    1979   *Text and Texture: Close Readings of Selected Biblical Texts* (New York: Schocken Books)
    1982   'Jewish Biblical Exegesis: Presuppositions and Principles', in Frederick E. Greensphan (ed.), *Scripture in the Jewish and Christian Traditions: Authority, Interpretation and Relevance* (Nashville: Abingdon)
    1985   *Biblical Interpretation in Ancient Israel* (Oxford: Clarendon Press)
    1989   *The Garments of Torah: Essays in Biblical Hermeneutics* (Bloomington: Indiana University)

Fowl, Stephen E. and L. Gregory Jones
    1991   *Reading in Communion: Scripture and Ethics in Christian Life* (Grand Rapids, Michigan: William B. Eerdmans)

Fowler, Roger
    1986   *Linguistic Criticism* (Oxford: Oxford University Press)

Frei, Hans W.
    1974   *The Eclipse of Biblical Narrative: a Study in Eighteen and Nineteen Century Hermeneutics* (New Haven: Yale University Press)

Gadamer, Hans-Georg
    1965   *Warheit und Methode Grundzuge einer Philosophichen Hermeneutik* 2nd edn; Tübingen: Mohr [ET *Truth and Method* (New York: Seabury 1975])

Giese, Ronald L.
    1995   'Literary Forms of the Old Testament,' in D. Brent Sandy
            & Ronald L. Giese (eds), *Cracking Old Testament Codes:
            A Guide to Interpreting the Literary Genres of the Old
            Testament* (Nashville, Tennessee: Broadman & Holman
            Publishers):5–27

Goldingay, John
    1994   *Models for Scripture* (Grand Rapids: Wm B. Eerdmans)

Gomes, Peter J.
    1996   *The Good Book: Reading the Bible with Mind and Heart*
            (New York: William Morrow and Company)

Goosen, D. P
    1996   'The Rhetoric of Scapegoat: A Deconstructive View on
            Postmodern Hermeneutics', in Stanley E. Porter and Tho-
            mas H. Olbricht (eds), *Rhetoric, Scripture and Theology*
            (JSNTSup, 131; England: Sheffield)

Graddol, David
    1994   'What is a Text,' in David Graddol and Oliver Boyd-Barrett
            (eds), *Media Texts: Authors and Readers* (Clevedon, En-
            gland: Multilingal Matters, Open University): 40–50

Greenberg, Moshe
    1957   'The Stabilization of the Text of the Hebrew Bible Reviewed
            in the Light of the Biblical Materials from the Judean Desert',
            Journal of the American Oriental Society 76:157–167

Greenstein, E.
    1988   'On the Genesis of the Biblical Prose Narrative' *Prooftexts*
            8: 347–354

Grenz, Stanley J.
    1995   'Star Trek and the Next Generation: Postmodernism and
            the Future of Evangelical Theology,' in David S. Dockery
            (ed), *The Challenge of Postmodernism: An Evangelical
            Engagement* (Wheaton, Illinois, 1995): 89–103
    1996   *A Primer on Postmodernism* (Grand Rapids, Michigan:
            Wm B. Eerdmans)

Halivni, David Weiss
    1991   *Peshat and Derash: Plain and Applied Meaning in Rab-
            binic Exegesis* (Oxford: Oxford University Press)

Halliday, M.A.K. and R. Hasan
    1976   *Cohesion in English* (London: Longman)

Harris, Wendell V.
    1991   'Canonicity', *PMLA* 106:110–121

Hawthorn, Jeremy
    1987   *Unlocking the Text: Fundamental Issues in Literary
            Theory* (London: Edward Arnold Publication)
    1994   *A Concise Glossary of Contemporary Literary Theory*
            (London: Edward Arnold)

Hayes, Richard B.
    1997   'Salvation by Trust? Reading the Bible faithfully', *Christian
            Century* 26 (1997):218–223

Hayman, Peter
    1995   'The Original Text:A Scholarly Illusion? in Jon Davies, Gra-
            ham Harvey and Wilfred G. E. Watson (eds),*Words Re-
            membered, Texts Renewed: Essays in Honour of John
            F. A. Sawyer* (JSOTSup 195; Sheffield:Sheffield Academic
            Press):434–449

Heidegger, Martin
    1927   'Sein und Zeit', in E. Husserl (ed.), *Jahrbuch fur
            Phanomenologie und Phanomenologishe Forschung*, VII
            (ET *Being and Time* [trans. J. Macquarrie and Edward
            Robinson; London: SCM, 1962])

Henry, Carl F.
    1995   'Postmodernism: The New Spectre,' in David S. Dockery
            (ed), *The Challenge of Postmodernism: An Evangelical
            Engagement* (Wheaton, Illinois, 1995):34–52

Hirsch, E. D.
    1967   *Validity in Interpretation* (New Haven: Yale University
            Press)

Holladay, Carl R.
  1994   'Contemporary Methods of Bible Reading', in Leander E.
          Keck, Thomas Long, et al. (eds), *The New Interpreters'
          Bible* (Nashville: Abingdon, 1994)
  1995   *The Interpretation of the Bible* (London: SCM)

Jeanrond, Werner G.
  1982   'Biblical Interpretation as Appropriation of Texts', in Wilfred
          Harington (ed), *Proceedings of the Irish Biblical Associa-
          tion* No.6 (Dublin: Irish Biblical Association)
  1988   *Text and Interpretation as Categories of Theological
          Thinking* (trans. Thomas J. Wilson; New York: Crossroad)
  1991   *Theological Hermeneutics* (London: SCM)
  1992   'Biblical Criticism and Theology: Towards a New Biblical
          Theology', *Journal of Literature and Theology* 6/3:218–
          227
  1993   'After Hermeneutics:The Relationship Between Theology
          and Biblical Studies,' in Francis Watson (ed), *The Open
          Text* (London: SCM)

Johnston, Robert Everard C.
  1977   *Text-Oriented Approach: Text Interpretation in the
          Thought of Paul Ricoeur* (Licentiate Dissertation,
          Katholieke Universiteit te Leuven)

Juhl, P. D.
  1980   *Interpretation: An Essay in Philosophy of Criticism*
          (Princeton: Princeton University Press)

Kaiser, C. Walter and Moíses Silva
  1994   *An Introduction To Biblical Hermeneutics: The Search
          For Meaning* (Grand Rapids, Michigan: Zondervan)

Keegan, Terence J.
  1985   *Interpreting the Bible: A Popular Introduction to Bibli-
          cal Hermeneutics* (New Jersey: Paulist)
  1995   'Biblical Criticism and the Challenge of Postmodernism',
          Biblical Interpretation 3:1–14

Klein, William W., Craig L. Bloomberg and Robert Hubbard, Jr.
  1993   *Introduction to Biblical Interpretation* (Dallas: Word Pub-
          lishing)

Knierim, Rolf P.
    1992   *Text and Concept in Leviticus 1:1–9* (Tübingen: J.C.B.
            Mohr [Paul Siebeck])

Koivsto, Rex A.
    1993   *One Lord, One Faith* (Wheaton, Ill: Victor Books)

Kort, Wesley A.
    1988   *Story, Text and Scripture: Literary Interests in Biblical
            Narrative* (University Park: The Pennsylvania State Uni-
            versity Press)

Kuhn, Thomas S.
    1970   *The Structure of Scientific Revolutions* (Chicago: Uni-
            versity of Chicago Press)

Lategan, Bernard C.
    1992   s.v. ' Hermeneutics', in *Anchor Bible Dictionary* (vol. 3;
            New York: Doubleday)149–154

Leitch, Vincent B.
    1983   *Deconstructive Criticism: An Advanced Introduction*
            (London: Hutchinson)

Letis, Theodore
    1991   'Brevard Childs and the Protestant Dogmatism: A Window
            to a New Paradigm in Biblical Interpretation', *Churchman*
            3:211–277

Levenson, Jon D.
    1993   *The Hebrew Bible: The Old Testament and Historical
            Criticism* (Louisville, Kentucky: Westminster/John Knox)

Lewis, C. S.
    1961   *An Experiment in Criticism* (Cambridge: Cambridge Uni-
            versity Press)

Lighstone, Jack N.
    1979   'The formation of the Biblical Canon in Judaism of Late
            Antiquity: Prolegomena to General Reassessment', *Sciences
            Religieuses* 8/2:135–142

Lim, Johnson. T. K
    1997   *The Sin of Moses and the Staff of God: A Narrative Approach* (Studia Semitica Neerlandica,35; Assen, The Netherlands: Van Gorcum)

Lints, Richard
    1993   *The Fabric Of Theology: A Prolegomenon To Evangelical Theology* (Grand Rapids, Michigan: Wm B. Eerdmans)

Lochhead, D.
    1977   'Hermeneutics and Theology', *The Ecumenist* 15:83–84
    1979   'A Reply to Responses', *Sciences Religieuses* 8/4:397–400

Longman III, Tremper
    1987   *Literary Approaches to Biblical Interpretation* (Grand Rapids Michigan: Zondervan Publishing House)

Long, Thomas G.
    1987   'Committing Hermeneutical Heresy', *Theology Today* XLIV/2:165–169

Long, V. Philips
    1994   *The Art of Biblical History* (FCI 5; Leicester: Apollos)

Lotman, Juriz
    1977   *The Structure of Artistic Text* (trans. Gail Lenhoff and Ronald Vroon; Ann Arbor; University of Michigan)

Loughlin, Gerard
    1995   'Using Scripture: Community and Letterality', in Jon Davies, Graham Harvey and Wilfred G. E. Watson (eds), *Words Remembered, Texts Renewed: Essays in Honour of John F. A. Sawyer* (JSOTSup 195; Sheffield:Sheffield Academic Press):321–339

Lundin, Roger
    1991   'Hermeneutics', in Clarence Walhout and Leland Ryken (eds.), *Contemporary Literary Theory: A Christian Appeal* (Grand Rapids Michigan: Eerdsman) 149–171
    1993   *The Culture of Interpretation* (Grand Rapids, Michigan: Wm B. Eerdmans)

Lund, Roger
    1991   'Hermeneutics', in Clarence Walhout and Leland Ryken
            (eds.), *Contemporary Literary Theory: A Christian Ap-
            peal* (Grand Rapids Michigan: Eerdmans)

Lyotard, F.
    1984   *The Postmodern Condition: A Report on Knowledge*
            (trans. Geoff Bennington and Brian Massumi; Minneapolis:
            University of Minnesota Press)

Mackie, Annebeth
    1968   *The Bible Speaks Again* (London: SCM)

Maier, Gerhard
    1994   *Biblical Hermeneutics* (trans. Robert W. Yarborough;
            Wheaton: Crossway Books)

Mazzeo, Joseph A.
    1978   *Varieties of Interpretation* (Notre Dame: University of
            Notre Dame)

McCarthy, John
    1992   s.v. 'Hermeneutics', in *A Handbook of Christian Theol-
            ogy* (Cambridge: Lutterworth) 219–224

McCarthy, Dan and Charles Clayton
    1994   *Let the Reader understand* (Illinois: Victor Books)

McEvenue, Sean
    1994   *Interpretation and Bible: Essays on Truth in Literature*
            (Collegeville, Minnesota: The Liturgical Press)

McGann, Jerome J.
    1983   *A Critique of Modern Textual Criticism* (London: Uni-
            versity of Chicago)

McKim, Donald K. (ed.)
    1986   *A Guide to Contemporary Hermeneutics: Major Trends
            in Biblical Interpretation* (Grand Rapids Michigan:
            Eerdmans)

McKnight, Edgar V.
    1993   'Reader Response Criticism' in Steven L. McKenzie and
            Stephen R. Haynes (eds.), *To Each Its Own Meaning* (Lon-
            don: Geoffrey Chapman) 197–220

Meyer, Ben F.
    1991   'The Challenge of Text and Reader to Historical Critical
            Method', in Wim Benken, Sean Fryne and Anton Weiler
            (eds), in *The Bible and Its Readers* (London: SCM Press)

Millar, John W.
    1994   *The Origins of the Bible: Rethinking Canon History* (New
            York: Paulist)

Millard, A. R
    1982   'In Praise of Ancient Scribes', *Biblical Archaeologist*
            45:143–153

Millar, J. Hillis
    1987   *The Ethics Of Reading* (New York: Columbia University
            Press)

Moberly, R. W. L.
    1983   *At the Mountain of God: Story and Theology in Exodus
            32–34* (JSOTSup, 22; Sheffield: JSOT Press)

Moore, Stephen D.
    1989   *Literary Criticism and the Gospels: The Theoretical
            Challenge* (New Haven: Yale University Press)
    1994   *Poststructuralism and the New Testament: Derrida and
            Foucault at the Foot of the Cross* (Minneapolis: Fortress)

Morgan, Donn F.
    1990   *Between Text and Community* (Minneapolis: Fortress
            Press)

Morgan, Robert and John Barton
    1989   *Biblical Interpretation* (Oxford: Oxford University Press)

Mulder, Martin Jan, (ed)
    1988   *Mikra: Text, Translation, Reading and Interpretation of
            the Hebrew Bible in Ancient Judaism and Early Chris-
            tianity* (Assen/Maastricht: Van Gorcum)

Mullen, E. Theodore
    1997   *Ethnic Myths and Pentateuchal Foundations* (Atlanta,
            Georgia: Scholars Press)

Nash, Roland H.
    1982   *The Word of God and the Mind of Man* (Grand Rapids:
            Zondervan)

Newton, Adam Zachary
1995   *Narrative Ethics* (Cambridge, Massachusetts: Harvard University Press)

Newton, K. M.
1986   *In Defense of Literary Interpretation* (London: Macmillan)
1990   *Interpreting the Text* (London: Harvester Wheatsheaf)

Noble, Paul R.
1991   *The Canonical Hermeneutics of Brevard Childs* (PhD dissertation, University of Cambridge)
1993   'Synchronic and Diachronic Approaches to Biblical Interpretation', *Journal of Literature and Theology* 7/2:130–148
1994   'Hermeneutics and Post-Modernism: Can we have a Radical Reader Response Theory? Part 1', in *Religious Studies* 31 (1995):419–436
1995   'Hermeneutics and Post-Modernism: Can we have a Radical Reader Response Theory? Part II', in *Religious Studies* 31 (1995):1–22

Noll, Stephen F.
1993   'Reading the Bible as the Word of God', in Frederick Houk Borsch (ed.), *The Bible's Authority in Today's Church* (Valley Forge, Penn: Trinity):133–168

Osborne, Grant R.
1991   *The Hermeneutical Spiral: A Comprehensive Introduction to Biblical Interpretation* (Illinois: Intervarsity)

Palmer, Richard E.
1969   *Hermeneutics: Interpretation Theory on Schleiermacher, Dilthey, Heidegger and Gadamer* (Evanston: Northwestern University Press)

Patte, Daniel
1995   *Ethics of Biblical Interpretation* (Louisville, Kentucky: Westminster/John Knox)

Perdue, Leo
1994   *The Collapse of History: Reconstructing Old Testament Theology* (OBT; Minneapolis: Fortress)

Pinnock, Clark H.
: 1984   *The Scripture Principle* (San Francisco: Harper and Row Publishers)

Poland, Lynn M.
: 1981   *Literary Criticism and Biblical Hermeneutics: A Critique of Formalist Approaches* (PhD Dissertation, University of Chicago)

Porter, Stanley E.
: 1990   'Why hasn't Reader Response Criticism caught on in New Testament Studies?' *Journal of Literature and Theology* 4/3:278–292

Poythress, Vern S.
: 1988   *Science and Hermeneutics* (Grand Rapids: Zondervan)

Provan, Iain
: 1997   'Canons to the Left of Him: Brevard Childs, His Critics, and the Future of Old Testament Theology' *Scottish Journal of Theology* 50/1:1–38

Quinn, Kenneth
: 1992   *How Literature Works* (London: MacMillan)

Ratzinger, Joseph Cardinal
: 1994   *The Interpretation of the Bible in the Church* (trans. John Kilgallen and Brendan Byrne; Quebec: Editions Paulines)

Reichert, John
: 1977   *Making Sense of Literature* (Chicago: University of Chicago)

Rendtorff, Rolf
: 1983   *Das Alte Testament: Eine Einfuhrung* (Neukirchener Verlag; ET *The Old Testament: An Introduction* [Philadelphia: Fortress Press, 1991])
: 1991   *Kanon und Theologie: Vorarbeiten zu einer Theologie des Alten Testaments* (Neukirchener Verlag; ET *Canon and Theology: Overtures to an Old Testament Theology* [Edinburgh: T. & T. Clark, 1994])
: 1993a   *Canon and Theology* (trans. Margaret Kohl; Minneapolis: Fortress Press)

1993b   'The Paradigm is Changing: Hopes and Fears', *Biblical Interpretation* 1 (1993): 34–52

1994   'Canonical Interpretation—A New Approach to Biblical Texts', *Studia Theologica* 48:3–14

1997   'Approaches to Old Testament Theology' in Henry T. C. Sun and Keith L. Eades (eds), *Problems in Biblical Theology: Essays in Honor of Rolf Knierim* (Grand Rapids: Eerdmans)

1998   'What We Miss by Taking the Bible Apart', in *Biblical Review* vol 14/1:42–44

Robinson, Robert Bruce
1988   *Roman Catholic Exegesis since Divino Afflante Spiritu: Hermeneutical Implications* (Atlanta, Georgia: Scholars Press)

Rowland, Christopher
1995   'The "Interested" Interpreter', in M. Daniel Caroll R., David J. A. Clines and Philip R. Davies (eds), *The Bible in Human Society: Essays in Honour of John Rogerson* (JSOTSup, 200; Sheffield: Sheffield Academic Press):429–444

Ryken, Leland and Tremper Longman III
1993   *A Complete Literary Guide to the Bible* (Grand Rapids, Michigan: Zondervan Publishing House)

Ryou, Daniel Hojoon
1995   *Zephaniah's Oracles against the Nations: A Synchronic and Diachronic Study of Zephaniah 2:1–3:8* (BIS 13; Leiden: E. J. Brill) Michigan: Zondervan Publishing House)

Sailhamer, John H.
1986   'Exegesis of the Old Testament as a Text', in Walter C. Kaiser and Ronald Youngblood (eds), *A Tribute to Gleason Archer* (Chicago: Moody Press): 279–296

1992   *The Pentateuch as Narrative* (Grand Rapids, Michigan: Zondervan)

1995   *Introduction to Old Testament Theology: A Canonical Approach* (Grand Rapids, Michigan: Zondervan)

Sanders, James A.
1995   'Scripture as Canon for Post-Modern Times', *Biblical Theology Bulletin* 25/2: 56–64

Sawyer, John
  1972   *Semantics in Biblical Research: New Methods of Defin-*
          ing Hebrew words for Salvation (London:SCM)

Schiffman, Lawerence H.
  1994   *Reclaiming the Dead Sea Scrolls* (Philadelphia: Jewish
          Publication Society)

Schnabel, Eckhard
  1995   'History, Theology and the Biblical Canon: An Introduc-
          tion to Basic Issue', in *Themelios* 20/2: 16–24

Schneiders, Sandra M.
  1991   *The Revelatory Text* (New York: Harper Collins)
  1993   'Scripture as the Word of God', The Princeton Seminary
          Bulletin XIV/1:18–35

Schökel, Alonso
  1974   'Hermeneutical Problems of a Literary study of the Bible',
          Supplements to the Vetus Testamentum 28:1–15
  1975   'Hermeneutical Problems of a Literary Study of the Bible',
          in G. W. Anderson, *Congress Volume, Edinburgh 1974*
          (Leiden: E. J. Brill)
  1985   'Of Methods and Models,' *Supplements to Vetus Testa-*
          mentum 36:3–13

Scholes, Robert
  1985   *Textual Power* (New Haven: Yale University Press)

Silva, Moises
  1987   *Has the Church Misread the Bible?* (Grand Rapids:
          Zondervan)
  1983   *Biblical Words and their Meaning: An Introduction to*
          Lexical Semantics (Grand Rapids, Michigan: Zondervan).

Smart, James
  1961   *The Interpretation of Scripture* (London: SCM Press)

Stanton, Graham
  1977   'Presuppositions in New Testament Criticism', in I. Howard
          Marshall (ed.), *New Testament Interpretation: Essays on*
          Principles and Methods (Exeter: Paternoster): 60–74

Stein. Robert H.
    1994   *Playing by the Rules* (Grand Rapids, Michigan: Baker
            Books)

Steiner, George
    1989   *Real Presences* (London: Faber and Faber)

Sternberg, Meir
    1985   *The Poetics of Biblical Narrative: Ideological Literature
            and the Drama of Reading* (Bloomington: Indiana Univer-
            sity Press)

Stott, John
    1992   *The Contemporary Christian : An Urgent Appeal for
            Double Listening* (Intervarsity Press)

Stuhlmacher, Peter
    1979   *Historical Criticism and Theological Interpretation of
            Scripture Towards a Hermeneutics of Consent* (trans.
            Roy A. Harrisville; London: SPCK)

Sundberg, Albert C.
    1964   *The Old Testament of the Early Church* (Cambridge, Mass
            and London)

Suppe, F. (ed.)
    1973   'Second Thoughts on Paradigm', in *The Structure of Sci-
            entific Theories* (Urbana: University of Illinois Press)

Tate, W. Randolph
    1991   *Biblical Interpretation: An Integrated Approach* (Peabody,
            Massachussetts: Hendrickson)

Thiselton, Anthony
    1980   *The Two Horizons: New Testament Hermeneutics and
            Philosophical Description with Special Reference to
            Heidegger, Bultmann, Gadamer and Wittgenstein*
            (Exeter: Paternoster Press)
    1992   *New Horizons in Hermeneutics* (Grand Rapids: Zondervan)

Topping, Richard
    1992   'The Canon and Truth: Brevard Childs and James Barr on
            the Canon and the Historical Critical Method', *Toronto
            Journal of Theology* 8:239–260

Todorov, Tzvetan
  1981   *Introduction to Poetics* (Great Britain: The Harvester Press
          Ltd)

Tov, Emanuel
  1981   *The Text Critical Use of the Septuagint in Biblical Re-
          search* (Jerusalem: Simor)
  1992   *Textual Criticism of the Hebrew Bible* (Minneapolis: For-
          tress Press, revised and enlarged edition of Biqqoret Nusah
          ha Mikra'-Piqê Mabo [Mosa Bialik: Jerusalem, 1989])
  1995   'Groups of Biblical Texts found at Qumran', in Devorah
          Dimant and Lawerence H. Schiffman (eds), *Time to Pre-
          pare the Way in the Wilderness* (Leiden: E. J. Brill):85–
          102

Tracy, David
  1975   *Blessed Rage for Order: The New Pluralism in Theology*
          (New York: The Seabury Press)
  1981   *The Analogical Imagination and the Culture of Plural-
          ism* (London: SCM)

Ulrich, Eugene C.
  1992a   'The Septuagint Manuscripts from Qumran: a Reappraisal
          of their value' in George J. Brooke and Barnabas Lindars
          (eds) *Septuagint, Scrolls and Cognate Writings* (Atlanta,
          Georgia: Scholars Press) 49–80
  1992b   'The Canonical Process, Textual Criticism, and Later Stages
          in the Composition of the Bible', in Michael Fishbane,
          Emanuel Tov (eds), Sha'arei Talmon: *Studies in the Bible,
          Qumran, and the Ancient Near East Presented to
          Shemaryahu Talmon* (Winona Lake, Indiana: Eisenbrauns)
  1994a   'The Bible in the Making: The Scriptures at Qumran', in
          Eugene Ulrich and James Vanderkam (eds), *The Commu-
          nity of the Renewed Covenant* (Notre Dame, Indiana:
          University of Notre Dame Press)
  1994b   'An Index of the passages in the Biblical Manuscripts from
          the Judean Desert (Genesis to Kings)', in *Dead Sea Dis-
          coveries* 1/1: 113–129

Valdes, Mario and Owen J. Miller (eds)
  1978   *Interpretation of Narrative* (Canada: Toronto University
          Press)

Van Dijk, Teun A.
1972   *Some Aspects of Grammar: A Study in Theoretical Linguistics and Poetics* (The Hague, Paris: Mouton)

Van Wolde, Ellen
1994   *Words Become Flesh: Semantic Studies of Genesis 1–11* (Leiden: E. J. Brill)

Van de Woude, Adam S.
1995   'Tracing the Evolution of the Hebrew Bible', *Bible Review* 11/1 :42–45

Vanhoozer, Kevin
1986   'The Semantics of Biblical Literature', in D. A. Carson and John Woodbridge (eds), *Hermeneutics, Authority and Canon* (Grand Rapids: Zondervan):52–104
1993   'The Hermeneutics of I-Witness Testimony: John 21:20–24 and the "Death" Of The "Author"' in A. Graeme Auld (ed.), *Understanding Poets and Prophets: Essays in Honour of George Wishart Anderson* (JSOTSup,152 Sheffield: JSOT) 366–387
1995a   'The Reader in New Testament Interpretation', in Joel B. Green (ed), *Hearing the New Testament: Strategies for Interpretation* (Grand Rapids, Michigan: Wm B. Eerdmans):301–328
1995b   'Exploring the World; Following the Word: The Credibility of Evangelical Theology in An Incredulous Age,' *Trinity Journal* 16:3–27

Wall, Robert W.
1995   'Reading the New Testament in Canonical Context', in Joel B. Green (ed), *Hearing the New Testament* (Grand Rapids, Michigan: William B. Eerdmans)

Watson, Francis (ed.)
1993   *The Open Text: New Direction for Biblical Studies* (London:SCM)
1994   *Text, Church and World: Biblical Interpretation in Theological Perspective* (Edinburgh: T & T Clark) Waugh, Patricia (ed)
1992   *Postmodernism, A Reader* (London: Edward Arnold)

Webster, Roger
  1990   *Literary Theory: An Introduction* (London: Edward
          Arnold)

Wellek, Rene and Austin Warren
  1973   *Theory of Literature* (Harmondsworth: Penguin)

Wenham, Gordon
  1989   'The Place of Biblical Criticism in Theological Study,'
          Themelios 14/4: 84–89

Widdowson, H. G.
  1983   *Learning Purposive and Language Use* (Oxford: Oxford
          University Press)

Wilkinson, Loren
  1996   'Hermeneutics and the Postmodern Reaction Against
          "Truth"'in Elmer Dyck (ed), *The Act of Bible Reading* (UK:
          Paternoster)

Wilson, Walter
  1993   *The Architectronics of Meaning: Foundations of the New
          Pluralism* (Chicago: The University of Chicago Press)

Wimsatt Jr, W.K.
  1954   *The Verbal Icon* (Lexington: University of Kentucky Press)

Wimsatt, W.K and M.C. Beardsley
  1946   'The Intentional Fallacy' *The Sewanee Review* LIV:468–
          487

Wood, Charles M.
  1981   *The Formation of Christian Understanding* (Valley Forge,
          PA: Trinity)
  1987   'Hermeneutics and the Authority of Scripture', in Garett
          Green (ed.), *Scriptural Authority and Narrative Interpre-
          tation* (Philadelphia: Fortress)
  1993   *The Formation of Christian Understanding* (Valley Forge;
          Trinity Press International)

Woodard, B. L. & Michael E. Travers
  1995   'Literary Forms and Interpretation,' in D. Brent Sandy &
          Ronald L. Giese (eds), *Cracking Old Testament Codes: A*

Guide to Interpreting the Literary Genres of the Old Testament (Nashville, Tennessee: Broadman & Holman Publishers):29–43

Wurthein, Ernst
    1979   *The Text of the Old Testament* (Trans. Eroll F. Rhodes; Grand Rapids, Michigan: Wm B. Eerdmans, repr.[1992])

Young, Frances
    1990   *The Art of Performance: Towards a Theology Of Holy Scripture* (London: Darton, Longman and Todd)

Young, Francis and David F. Ford
    1987   *Meaning and Truth in 2 Corinthians* (London: SPCK)

Ziesler, John
    1994   'Historical Criticism and a Rational Faith', *Expository Times* 105/9:270–274

Studies in Biblical Literature

This series invites manuscripts from scholars in any area of biblical literature. Both established and innovative methodologies, covering general and particular areas in biblical study, are welcome. The series seeks to make available studies that will make a significant contribution to the ongoing biblical discourse. Scholars who have interests in gender and sociocultural hermeneutics are particularly encouraged to consider this series.

For further information about the series and for the submission of manuscripts, contact:

Hemchand Gossai
Department of Religion
Muhlenberg College
2400 Chew Street
Allentown, PA 18104-5586

To order other books in this series, please contact our Customer Service Department:

(800) 770-LANG (within the U.S.)
(212) 647-7706 (outside the U.S.)
(212) 647-7707 FAX

or browse online by series at:

WWW.PETERLANGUSA.COM